难民

NÀNMÍN

Concavity of China's Refugee Policy

PREETHI AMARESH

Notion Press

No.8, 3rd Cross Street,
CIT Colony, Mylapore,
Chennai, Tamil Nadu – 600004

First Published by Notion Press 2021
Copyright © Preethi Amaresh 2021
All Rights Reserved.

ISBN
Hardcase: 978-1-63745-461-9
Paperback: 978-1-63745-437-4

In fond memory of…

Shri. Kotha. Amareshwara Rao
My Late Father

Contents

Acknowledgement 7

Foreword..9

Acronyms 11

Chapter1: The Refugee Upheaval in the 21ˢᵗ Century - Prologue......13

Chapter2: The Refugee Policy of China 19

Chapter3: UNHCR in the Chinese Soup................................23

Chapter4: The Indo-Chinese Refugee Haywire 29

Chapter5: The Syria Dilemma 35

Chapter6: The Tibet Enigma 41

Chapter7: The Invisible Refugees of North Korea 49

Chapter8: Xinjiang on the Big Plate – "Sinicisation" of Islam........55

Chapter9: The Slow Asphyxiation of the Kachins 69

Chapter10: The Forgotten Kokangs 77

Chapter11: The Rohingya Fiasco 83

Chapter12: Hong Kong in a Cleft Stick 89

Chapter13: The COVID Pandemic Dust An Epilogue 97

References...105

Index 115

Acknowledgement

Writing a book is assiduous and it definitely demands a lot of time and patience. The year 2020 has been a testing time for humanity due to COVID-19, which is still at the tipping point for the pandemic dust to settle down. Nevertheless, It feels great winding up 2020 with my second international book release titled "Nanmin", which means "Refugee" in Mandarin Chinese language. I began writing this book in 2017 while I was working for the United Nations High Commissioner for Refugees (UNHCR), India, which I finally decided to finish in 2020 and I would like to thank all the people in the acknowledgement for being involved in this journey.

I would like to convey my sincere thanks to Mr. Karthikeyan M, Special Government Pleader & Advocate (High court of Madras, India) & likewise a renowned author of several books and Mr. Senthil Kumar, Pearson Indian author for the continuous guidance and encouragement throughout the book.

I would like to express my gratitude to Dr. Srikanth Kondapalli, a renowned writer and commentator quoted regularly in the national & international media, a leading Indian expert on China and the former Chairperson of Centre for East Asian Studies (Jawaharlal Nehru University, New Delhi) for writing the foreword and reviewing my book.

I feel grateful to my mother Shyla Amaresh, sister Swetha Amaresh, brother-in-law Dr. Shailesh from Australia for always being a constant support and my nephew Sravan and niece Sraddha for being my all time cheerleaders.

I would like to thank my fiancée Capt. Sushanth, an Australian trained pilot from Tristar Aviation, Melbourne presently, serving as an International Pilot (Air India Express, Government of India) for all the love & support and for being so creative in suggesting the title "Nanmin" for the book.

Lastly, It was my pleasure working with the team of Notion Press and I thank the team for being so efficient in publishing my book on time.

– Preethi Amaresh

Foreword

While the phenomenon of the refugees is considered to be part of the "low politics" in the domain of security studies which has its focus mainly on the state security, post-Cold War period has thrown up the importance of the non-traditional security issues to the fore. The recent debates in Europe about the limits of multiculturalism, as West Asian and North African refugees made an influx, has further increased the spotlight on the refugee policies. Globalizations, political repression at home, rise of non-state actors' profile, pull and push economic factors to migrate and others are said to have triggered refugee flow.

China as one of the most populated countries in the world has contributed to the outflow of the over 40 million migrants to far flung areas abroad. Replacement of dynasties in history – like the Ming and the Qing – led to reprisals and migration thus contributing to the Overseas Chinese in Southeast Asia and other regions. Communist rule since 1949 further increased the outflow, mainly to Taiwan, Hong Kong and other regions.

As a multi-ethnic state and an authoritarian regime, China's refugee policy is complicated due to its rigid citizenship laws that emphasise on 同胞 (*tongbao* - born to the same womb), political suspicions about adjustments to the western nations policies, loss of face and others that test its claims to be a "responsible big country".

Apart from massive internal migration of 200 to 300 million people to the urban areas in search of employment, better health care and education, even as they were discriminated in housing, health care benefits, education and others either by the residents or municipal authorities, external migration to Siberia, Myanmar, India, Kazakhstan and other countries has created political problems with the neighborhood for China.

Specifically, its insistence on following "One China" policy and the "inalienability" clause in the joint statements with neighbors has caused concerns recently. China's paramilitary and police intrusions into Nepal in search of Tibetans or the Kokang in Myanmar have created tensions recently.

Ms. Preethi Amaresh explores the subject of China's refugee policy and its dynamics in a comprehensive manner in this book. She analyzed the refugee policy of China in 13 crisp chapters highlighting both how it has evolved and impacting on the neighborhood, touching upon important areas of Tibet, Xinjiang, Syria, Indochina, North Korea, Myanmar, Hong Kong and other regions.

Ms. Amaresh is intelligent, hardworking, energetic and capable of addressing such a complex topic given her training, extensive publications and acumen. I am sure this book will be helpful to policy makers, media, academics and the lay.

– Dr. Srikanth Kondapalli
A leading Indian expert on China and
the former Chairperson of Centre for East Asian Studies
(Jawaharlal Nehru University, New Delhi)

Acronyms

BRI	Belt and Road Initiative
BPL	Below Poverty Line
COVID	Coronavirus Disease
CPC	Communist Party of China
CPA	Comprehensive Plan of Action
CPB	Communist Party of Burma
ETLM	East Turkestan Liberation Movement
ECHR	The European Court of Human Rights
ETIC	East Turkistan Information Centre
Ex Com	Executive Committee
ETLO	Eastern Turkistan Liberation Organization
HKSAR	Hong Kong Special Administrative Region
HRW	Human Rights Watch
IDPs	Internally displaced persons
IO's	International Organizations
ICJ	International Court of Justice
ICCPR	International Covenant on Civil and Political Rights
ICESCR	International Covenant on Economic, Social and Cultural Rights
ICRC	International Committee of the Red Cross
KMT	Kuomintang
KWAT	Kachin Women's Association Thailand
KIO	Kachin Independence Organization
KIA	Kachin Independence Army
LAC	Line of Actual Control
MNDAA	Myanmar National Democratic Alliance Army
MWA	The Middle Way Approach
NGO	Non Government Organization

PRC	People's Republic of China
PAP	People's Armed Police
PLA	People's Liberation Army
RSD	Refugee Status Determinations
RATS	The Regional Anti-Terrorist Structure
SLORC	State Law and order Restoration Council
SCO	Shanghai Cooperation Organization
UNHCR	United Nations High Commissioner for Refugees
U.N	United Nations
UNSC	United Nations Security Council
UNRWA	United Nations Reliefs and Works Agency
UDHR	Universal Declaration of Human Rights
USM	Unified Screening Mechanism
UNGC	United Nations Convention on the Prevention and Punishment of the Crime of Genocide
UWSA	United WA State Army
UAE	United Arab Emirates
WUYC	World Uighur Youth Congress
WFP	World Food Program
WPK	Worker's Party of Korea
WHO	World Health Organization
XPCC	Xinjiang Production and Construction Corps

CHAPTER 1

The Refugee Upheaval in the 21st Century
Prologue

The refugee crisis is a universal stumbling block where almost every country is experiencing repercussions. There has been a cumbersome change in humanity. According to the United High Commissioner for Refugees (UNHCR), 65.6 million displaced people have been forcibly displaced globally because of conflict, environmental destruction, violence, human rights violations and persecution including 22.5 million refugees, 10 million stateless people, and only 189,300 resettled refugees as per 2017 report. This global refugee plight of the 21st century is viewed as the largest displacement of people ever since World War II. The extent of UNHCR has grown to encompass the security of internally displaced persons (IDPs). Diverse international events and conferences by the United Nations (U.N) and other organizations have helped to provide efficient solutions, new methods plus strategies to community projects, funding for philanthropic aid and new resettlement areas for refugees. The New York declaration by the U.N advocates in supporting more comprehensive rethinking of the connection between development, protection and mobility for the migrants and refugees. However, despite making great efforts, the international organizations, intergovernmental organizations, international treaties and laws and nation-states have been grappling hard to handle the massive crisis circumstances.

The refugee crisis exposes the cracks in the international order with the continued displacement to uncertainty, painful waste of human resources and potential, disorder and financial disruption where millions of people are ensnared in a predicament of a lingering yoke for ages. A refugee has been defined, as "A refugee is someone who has been forced to flee his or her country because of persecution, war or violence. A refugee has a well-founded fear of persecution for reasons of race, religion, nationality, political opinion or membership in a particular social group. Most likely, they cannot return home or are afraid to do so. War and ethnic, tribal and religious violence are leading causes of refugees fleeing their countries". Loescher, In 'Refugee and International Relations', notes that, "Government responses to refugee movements from neighboring or distant nations are considerably influenced by the relations between sending and receiving nations." When inhabitants decide to escape a nation, in principle, this signifies a breakdown of the nation-state, as it is incapable to provide its citizens economic, political, or societal security. Refugees at present are finding it more finicky to find refuge in advanced nations and refugee flows among the developing nations are growing at a high pace across the world. The outcomes of refugee flows are transnational, and due to these changes, there is a potential to imperil global security.

The international refugee regime was formed to support global stability by building suitable foundations to respond to refugee outflows. The refugee regime is essentially connected to the fundamentals of the nation-state that is postulated on the most primary role and accountability of the state to grant protection and shelter to its occupants. Many of the refugees today have been an outcome of long-ago conflicts. The conception of the State of Israel in 1948 affected thousands of Palestinians to escape to bordering nations. Another outpouring of Palestinians befell at the course of the Six-Day War in 1967. Collectively they make up one of the most populous refugee society in the world. The therapeutic amenities of Gaza have frequently been targeted by the Israeli air force, and the people must now depend on primeval hospitals and dispensaries for their continuance. The Palestinians suffered another severe blow when U.S. President Donald Trump chose to annul American funding for the United Nations Relief and Works Agency (UNRWA) for Palestine Refugees, which has further put Palestinian lives at jeopardy. Another important refugee movement was in 1950 when the Tibetans escaped to India along with their spiritual leader, His Holiness Dalai Lama when it was invaded and seized by China. The presence of the Dalai Lama in India is the cause of continuous disagreements between the governments of China and India.

As the fall of the Soviet Union took place in 1991, the international refugee regime was faced by a fresh contour of the global system. When developing nations in Asia and Africa started to achieve independence, civil uprisings provoked an outpouring of people seeking refugee in developed nations. Countries in the west started to sense the pressure in consolidating refugees into their communities, and the admission of the refugee grew more restrictive. Hence, the treatment of these groups wasn't the same.

In the 21st century, different natures of wars like terrorism and proxy wars presented grounds for global mediation to avert possible refugee movements. The Syria cataclysm after the war erupted in 2011 has been terrifying than any crisis in the world displacing over a million within 6 months as much as that of the Rohingya refugees. As per the present data, there are around 5.6 million Syrian refugees, apart from 6.2 million people who are uprooted within Syria. On the whole, nearly 12 million people in Syria need humanitarian support. In the second decade of the 21st century, refugees have scarce to look onward to. Repatriation is a far-flung hope for most, as the number of refugees who were able to return safely to their houses reached the flattest level in more than 30 years in 2015. Due to not much of international support, a vast number of refugees have taken the concerns within their cards leaving lands of the first asylum to nations like Europe or more flourishing countries. The large majority of refugees survive in countries of first asylum, usually for decades, breathing in the exploitation, poor governance and also sometimes lacking the basic facilities. Cultural, Social, religious and societal norms are impaired due to the refugee trauma.

Approximately two-thirds of the persecuted refugees are mainly from Somalia, Libya, Myanmar, Syria, Yemen, Ethiopia, South Sudan and Afghanistan and have experienced unimaginable loss and destruction. Likewise, countries such as Pakistan, Lebanon, Jordan, Turkey, South Africa and Palestine are home to almost 50 per cent of the world's asylum seekers and refugees. The displacement of more than a million expatriates in 2015 over the Mediterranean Sea led to long-needed thought to the flaw of the international humanitarian apparatus. It has also taken a toll on the destiny of the present generation children who encounter a tumultuous childhood and miss out on education or might end up having a long hiatus in education. The refugees are either displaced in their own country or move abroad for safety. The longing to return to home, people yearning to go back to work and their dreams for the future have been shattered and have left them in a state of a dilemma with an uncertain future. As per the foreign and state laws, many refugees who travel to different countries don't qualify for the refugee status. So, they end up travelling to escape the crunching poverty, fissiparous and corrupt governments and natural calamities. In these horrendous circumstances, refugees tend to get exploited while they experience furtive voyages. Narrow-minded national interests of various nations have thwarted the attempts to find a more humane and coordinated passageway to extensive movements of migrants and refugees.

The barriers within domestic unification, national security, and public safety concerns are eroding. International Organizations (IO's) such as the U.N, Amnesty International are requesting various countries to change their opinions to meet the refugee challenges. Amnesty International cautioned that even the phrase "responsibility-sharing" is in peril. The following organization criticizes the absence of governmental will and readiness to undergo the preventable misery of millions of people by advancing to build barricades. Salil Shetty, the former Secretary-General of Amnesty International states that, "Millions of refugees throughout the world are in urgent need where 86 per cent live in low and middle-income nations frequently ill-equipped to host them, while many of the world's wealthiest states host the fewest and do the least which is inherently unfair".

The contemporary preoccupation of our media with the COVID-19 crisis has left us ill informed about many other major write-ups on the global scene. The absolute totality of refugees across the world, and the circumstances under which most of them are compelled to live, shows a humanitarian catastrophe of unprecedented dimensions in the contemporary times. Refugees blend most strongly when there is a synergy between government and civil society to nurture social inclusion and forge ties between refugees and the people and institutions of their present societies. But when that synergy is lacking, anxiety and hostility can grow. When they are robust, refugees can add to the making of active communities. Turning these commitments into reality presents a major challenge for international cooperation.

Majority of the Chinese nationals dislike the U.N for many factors. China apprehends the financial cost of providing the refugee assistance that the UNHCR advocates. Allowing complete entree to the UNHCR could present China's ineffectual treatment of refugees. China would have no genuine act for it's functioning, and this observation could scatter over to China's record with its minority communities.

CHAPTER 2

The Refugee Policy of China

"China can help to stabilize areas in conflict and address the root causes of displacement."

– UNHCR

In the last few decades, People's Republic of China (PRC) has come to understand that they can remold the global system to conform to their national interests. China has been the second-largest economy in the world but its monetary grants to UNHCR does not seem to be proportionate with its economic strength. As its economic and military control has been expanding, it seeks leadership and admiration. Being one of the five permanent members of the UN Security Council (UNSC), China does not explicitly reject the UNHCR's weight for the concern of imperiling its UNSC veto. But, this does not also mean that China wholly complies with its mandate. With vital economic growth in contemporary years, the country is rising as a stop and transit nation for many refugees. Though China has maintained a friendly relationship with UNHCR, it has seldom vexed association with UNHCR and its preceding record of inadequate donations to UN agencies in general. In 2017, China has sharply raised its support for the UNHCR from $2.8 million to $12.5 million. Its yearly donation to UNHCR is however significantly lower as compared to the U.S or Japan. China was placed at 39th and 51st in terms of the amount of yearly donation to UNHCR, while the US and Japan ranked the first and the second in 2016 and 2015 respectively.

China has long been a significant source of asylum seekers and refugees. It has seldom been viewed as a refugee-receiving nation. For most of the 20th century, it was a source of refugees fleeing political repression, wars and civil conflicts. For instance, a large number of people fled to Hong Kong through the times of famine in 1959- 1961 led by Mao Zedong's "Great Leap Forward" and likewise by the violent "Cultural Revolution". Post the "Great Escape to Hong Kong", the economy of China steadily developed as it continued its reform and opening-up process in 1978. After China's legal status was restored in the U.N in 1971, the Executive Committee (Ex Com) of UNHCR had to terminate the membership of the Taiwan authorities in the year 1972.

As the "Open Door Policy", commenced in 1978, China sharing boundaries with various sovereign nations has steadily become a destination for refugees from overseas often due to its geographic vicinity and economic advancement. Since 1978, China has received around 283,000 Indo-Chinese refugees. In the year 1979, UNHCR signed a project agreement for assistance to the Indo-Chinese refugees in China. For the Burmese or Myanmar refugees, China has pursued a strategy to grant provisional relief by providing essential items, while nevertheless failing to accept them as refugees. Concerning North Korean refugees, China seeks a stringent policy to decline and repatriate North Koreans who are caught by Chinese authorities. China has also vigorously repatriated UNHCR refugees like in the case of 1992 where, the Chinese officials repatriated more than 30 UNHCR refugees. In June 2017, China's Foreign Minister, Wang Yi asserted that refugees from Syria and other countries would have to go back from China to their homelands as Beijing has come forward for financial support to nations that are struggling with global refugee crisis.

China, being a signatory to the 1951and 1961 United Nations Convention on refugees and migrants has also acceded to its 1967 Protocol in September 1982. However, the percentage of migrants and refugees China allowed is very little in comparison to its population and ability. At present the relevant provisions are article 32 of the Constitution and article 46 of the Exit and Entry Law. Article 32 provides the general principle on asylum where China may grant asylum to foreigners who request it for political reasons. Exit and Entry law provides that refugees and asylum seekers in China may obtain identity cards. According to Article 46 of 'The Exit and Entry Administration Law of the People's Republic of China', the Foreigners applying for refugee status during the screening process may stay in China on the strength of temporary identity certificates issued by public security organs. Foreigners who are recognized as refugees may stay in China on the strength of refugee identity certificates issued by public security organs.

There is an overall advancement of China's foreign policy and global approach, from Deng Xiaoping's "hiding brightness" to the "great renaissance" under Xi Jinping's administration. Performing a more consequential role at the U.N and in global governance more generally is currently a vital element of Xi's ambitious plan to drive China as a great power nation. In order to fully understand how China's foreign policy and refugee policy are related, one must first examine the definition of a "refugee," as well as the development of the international refugee regime. As per the cornerstone of China's foreign policy, China has decided to minimize her engagement in foreign turmoil as far as possible. China has no law or procedure for determining refugee status and the UNHCR has not been given access to conduct refugee status determinations (RSD) under international law where the lack of a formal recognition mechanism does not negate the fact that someone is a refugee. There is fluctuation in China's handling of each group in terms of the level of aid China provides. For instance, Following severe anti-Chinese tumults in Indonesia in 1998, for example, the Chinese state seemed loath to reach out with propositions of assistance to the victims, despite the urgency for an instantaneous and effective response from popular sentiment within China. Reports state that the Chinese prefer taking ethnic Chinese refugees rather than the outsiders. The "Political Ideology" of China's discouragement of acceptance of non-Chinese refugees is a factor to be highlighted. The UNHCR 2015 Fact Sheet revealed that China did not grant adequate support to refugees who were not ethnic Chinese who stayed in its regions on neither temporary nor permanent footing. The Chinese "Green Card" only provides a narrow path to being a resident of China. Even though China promotes the concept of ethnic diversity, it focuses on the symbiosis of the 56 ethnic groups recognized by the government.

With the new turn of "Globalization" in the post COVID world, the refugee issue will go beyond the political and diplomatic domain in China. It is also the loss or gain of global reputation that the Chinese government will have to consider while taking decisions on refugee policies. The mistreating refugees by China from neighboring lands could drive to not a just humanitarian catastrophe and global reputational damage, it can further cause great impairment to bilateral ties, geographical instability and insecurity.

CHAPTER 3

UNHCR in the Chinese Soup

> **"Globally, one in every 122 humans is now either a refugee, internally displaced or seeking asylum. Most alarmingly, over half the world's children are refugees."**
>
> **–UNHCR report**

UNHCR has been the sole organization that tackles refugee rights in China. It was in 1980 that UNHCR instituted an office in Beijing and has been handling refugee status requests since then. Since the last 40 years, UNHCR has been collaborating with China and vice-versa. China's contribution to refugees' aid as per the UNHCR report has grown from US$2.8 million in 2016 to US$12.5 million in 2017 because of the Belt and Road Initiative (BRI). The BRI at the global stage, which consists of people to people exchanges, investment, connectivity, trade and commerce, infrastructure has expanded to more than 60 nations in Asia, Africa and Europe, where refugees also exist. Filippo Grandi, UNHCR refugee chief, described China's capacity to the root movements of the refugee crises worldwide through various development initiatives. The UNHCR chief stated that China being the world's most populated nation is competent in doing more to discuss the root problems of displacement and aid with the global refugee emergencies through supporting economic advancement.

The UN Secretary-General report stated in 2016 that, 'All refugees and migrants, regardless of status, are entitled to due process of law in the determination of their legal status, entry and right to remain, and in no cases are collective expulsions permissible'. It is observed that more than 50 per cent of the global 10.5 million refugees under UNHCR's decree presently inhabit in cities and towns across the globe. The preferences in refugee policy have been economic security and self-sufficiency. Several come with just a suitcase, others arrived with nothing except their clothes. The UNHCR assists in terms of health care, food, accommodation and children's education. The UNHCR Chief, who affirmed that soft power represents an imperative in evolving stance towards the refugees, underscored the opportunism of China concerning soft power on refugees. Article 35 of the 1951 Refugee Convention and Article II of the 1967 Protocol impel states to cooperate with UNHCR in the performance of its objectives and to assist UNHCR to oversee the realization of the prerequisites in the Refugee Convention. According to the 1995 China–UNHCR Agreement, article 35 of the Refugee Convention requires States to collaborate with UNHCR in the operation of its purposes, as a basis of cooperation within the Chinese government and UNHCR. The government of China accepts the status of refugees established by UNHCR. However, it has had restricted engagement in the refugee status determination (RSD) process. China declared its statutory commitment to interact with UNHCR in its December 1, 1995 agreement asserting that "UNHCR personnel may at all times have unhampered access to refugees and to the places of UNHCR projects in order to observe all facets of their implementation".

Considering some provisions of the Refugee Convention and Protocol has been included into Chinese law and any Chinese law has not accepted the direct applicability of these two implements. Which means the Refugee Convention and Protocol are not directly applicable in China. So, due to this, the refugees are not able to take a case to a Chinese court to effectuate the provisions of the Refugee Convention and Protocol. Also, very few Chinese laws consider refugees or asylum. Chinese officials oftentimes dismiss UNHCR and other humanitarian institutions access to assess security needs or provide support to asylum seekers and people stuck in various other refugee-like circumstances. Refugees in China, even those accepted under UNHCR's mandate, have no legitimate status in China and cannot use Chinese courts to seek their rights except that they have a residence permit or approved visa. Under Chinese law, the government can arrest, detain, extradite or deport any economic migrant, asylum seeker or refugee. Judge Xue of the International Court of Justice (ICJ) asserted that the agreements ratified by China do not automatically become section of the Chinese national law and hence do not instinctively become "de jure" in China. Furthermore, the Chinese government usually gives limited money or social advantages for refugees whose status is accepted through the RSD mode governed by UNHCR. Overall, UNHCR refugees are treated as nonnatives who normally have no right to work or entree to public education and depend on the UNHCR for aid in terms of healthcare, accommodation and other essential needs. The detainment centers in

China are not directed to autonomous monitoring, and asylum seekers or refugees have no statutory power to confront their detainment in the judiciary.

China has signed mutual border management agreements with several neighbors where these agreements include stipulations associating to border residents and thus explain the phrase 'border residents' as nationals of each nation party or both States parties who reside in the boundary regions. Notwithstanding its commitments under international law, especially as a party to the Refugee Convention, there are no distinctive requirements in Chinese law to acknowledge refugees in China's frontiers. As per the 2016 statistics of UNHCR, there were nearly 3,17,923 enrolled refugees in China among which a bulk of registered refugees are ethnic Chinese from Vietnam who escaped to China in the late 1970s. When another humanitarian disaster-hit where sailboats carrying thousands of Rohingya arrived off Southeast Asian coasts, China did little possibly because the Rohingya are not ethnic Chinese. Most of these agreements also include distinctive propitious border-crossing settlements for eligible border residents, although the essence of the arrangements differs from one agreement to another.

UNHCR has been asking the world to stand together with refugees is through inviting well-known celebrities from various countries including China to present various narratives about refugees that people may not have heard. "For instance, Leah Dou a Chinese singer-songwriter told the tale of a young Syrian refugee woman called Yusra Mardini, who was once in a crowded boat in the Mediterranean and later became an Olympic swimmer. Mardini is presently also the youngest Goodwill Ambassador."

The year 2020 has been a challenging time for the world post-Pandemic. Nevertheless, it has been more testing for refugee and uprooted families being more vulnerable than ever in extraordinary circumstances. The pandemic has drastically decreased the availability of perpetual answers to long-term displacement. Many states across the world sealed their boundaries and blocked the way to refuge due to the spread of COVID. The pandemic has likewise taught us the value of working collectively with shared responsibilities. COVID has fired up a number of hurdles that have led to delays for refugee security. However, digital and innovative technologies have demonstrated to be extremely successful in increasing remote access to refuge systems apart from providing the refugees counseling services to deal with psychological stress of pandemic. The second-largest economy China, along with UNHCR must find opportunities for resettlement and voluntary repatriation and increase the economic aid, keeping in mind the inclusion of refugees. Where UNHCR buys one billion U.S. dollars of goods annually to assist and protect refugees globally, China suppliers should come forward to invest more in the quality relief items such as innovative services and commodities.

UNHCR since 1994, has focused on the aid plans for the refugees who are facing acute poverty and hardship by adopting the "revolving funds", a new method of management where the funds recovered from the projects will be reinvested in the work creating projects for the refugees. In this way, UNHCR should continue increasing the revolving funds for the refugees to create different employment opportunities for the ones who have lost their jobs due to COVID pandemic. A good synergy between China and UNHCR is necessary for proper treatment of various ethnic refugees and China should play a more constructive role in the area of international refugee relief. The UNHCR and Chinese authorities should first and foremost build trust with each other for a long-term engagement.

CHAPTER 4

The Indo-Chinese Refugee Haywire

The global refugee problem is evolving and reveals no indications of decline. The Indochina refugee trauma is considered to be a massive flow of people in 1975 from the previous French colonies of Indochina like Laos, Cambodia and Vietnam after communist regimes were instituted. Out of the total Indo Chinese population of 56 million, more than 3 million people took a treacherous route to become refugees in China, Hong Kong and South-East Asia in 1975.

China is regarded as the second-largest host land for Indo-Chinese refugees due to the innumerable number of refugees received since they are known to be ethnic Chinese. The Indochinese refugees consist essentially of four different ethnic groups namely Hmong, Cambodian, Vietnamese and Laotian. The largest group, the Vietnamese, is highly heterogeneous. These groups are heterogeneous in culture and history that is displayed by substantial variations in class background, educational achievement, religion, job and ethnicity. Indochinese refugees are a diverse society displaying many religions, cultures, nationalities and class settings. The Indochinese, are broadly considered as hard working and industrious labor with a longing for self-sufficiency but they have also at times encountered short term and long term underemployment following resettlement. Many are well educated by Vietnamese standards and show what was the country's cream or elite. However, Vietnamese and Hmong have been seen continuing in dire poverty with limited or no agency association but the appetite for the Indochinese to grow economically autonomous, nevertheless, has been exceptional, as they have jumped into the labor force immediately.

Global attention was brought to Indo Chinese refugees, especially by the situation of thousands of boat refugees. The "boat people" of Indo China presented a climactic illustration of a growing global crisis. The Vietnamese refugee crisis started with the "Fall of Saigon" in 1975 and the unrelenting actuality of the communist government, which ended in the mass emigration of "boat people" starting in 1978. Differences of political regimes in Cambodia, Vietnam and Laos in 1975 set off huge refugee migrations across South East Asia, that persists even now as an obstacle of both political and humanitarian matter to the U.S. Several Indo-Chinese refugees from Cambodia, Laos, Malaysia, Philippines, Vietnam, Indonesia and Hong Kong have moved to Chinese regions of Yunnan, Guangxi, Guangdong, Fujian, Jiangxi and Hainan. Some of these refugees who reside in China are considered a breakthrough story. China and UNHCR in 1979 signed the plan contract for support to the Indo-Chinese refugees in China. Almost 90% of the Indo-Chinese refugees have profited from these plans to different magnitude. Many of Indo-Chinese refugees are living a steady and comfortable life under the security of UNHCR and CPC. The Indo Chinese refugees have been provided with essential needs such as education, shelter, employment etc. though CPC had to spend a lot of its expense concerning their security. Nevertheless, the aid programs administered by UNHCR to China have performed a determining function. The UNHCR has attempted to expand global cooperation in easing the refugee crisis through the shifts in the international conferences and funding programs and to gain elevated resettlement offers. China has given adequate security to these refugees following the policy of fair treatment, equal remuneration and non-discrimination for equal work since last many decades. It has successfully taken nearly 3-lakh Vietnam citizens where they have created new lives in China, though many of them are still considered as refugees. Considering the time of the Indochinese migration, resettlement has been much more complicated and resource-intense and has additionally attained global legitimacy as it has become more sensitive to international security requirements.

China's policy towards refugees from Vietnam contracted by July 1978, when Sino-Vietnamese relations deteriorated and the burden of refugees had become so prominent that China sealed the frontier and started without success to emphasize that Vietnam take back most of the refugees. Later, following many years, China more unobtrusively expedited the travel to Hong Kong or Macao of some Vietnamese refugees who had been resettled in China. Anxieties were intensified following an international agreement known as the Comprehensive Plan of Action (CPA) that was ratified at a conference in Geneva held by "The Steering Committee of the International Conference on Indo-Chinese Refugees" in 1989 pointing to a focus on repatriation back to Vietnam for those considered not to be refugees. The

Philippines allowed to establish a regional processing hub for refugees bound for third nation resettlement and likewise presented first-asylum to Vietnamese Boat People. Numerous Laotians and Cambodians have fled for reasons alike to those of the Vietnamese. During the Cambodian Pol Pot regime, many thousands fled while over a million Cambodians were killed during this regime.

Refugee movements too remain to pose likely disruptive political intricacies for Southeast Asian countries of the first asylum like Singapore, Malaysia, Hong Kong, Thailand and Indonesia and test the strength of the UNHCR to deal adequately with this predicament. Barely a few nations like Australia, Japan, China, U.S, France and Canada helped alleviate the weight by admitting refugees for resettlement. Following the 1979 international conference on the Situation of Refugees and Displaced Persons in Southeast Asia, Japan turned out to be one of the world's biggest contributors to U.N relief programs for Indo-Chinese refugees. Each of these nations has served as a point of temporary refuge for Indo Chinese refugees.

Despite barely a tiny portion of refugees are resettled annually, resettlement has been given more prominent standing as a legitimate migration pathway in reply to some of the largest hurdles confronting the global protection regime. Following the end of World War II, roughly 1.6 million refugees have immigrated to the U.S and many of the migrants being the Indo Chinese. The resource funds for Indo-Chinese by the U.S estimated for approximately one billion U.S dollars through the end of 2000. Under Indo china Migration and Refugee Assistance Act passed in 1975 under U.S president Gerald Ford due to the Fall of Saigon and the end of the Vietnam war, the aforementioned act with nearly 130,000 refugees from South Vietnam, Laos and Cambodia were permitted to enter the U.S following a distinctive status where the act allotted for special relocation support and financial aid. The Orderly Departure Program from 1979 until 1994 promoted to resettle refugees in the U.S and other westbound nations.

As per the former UNHCR chief António Guterres, the Indo-Chinese experience has been one of the most successful integration programmes in the world. However, today the situation is different and refugees are entering much quicker than they can be resettled and first asylum nations worry that resettlement in third nations will be inefficient to maintain pace and will never incorporate all refugees. China's future unfoldings will be sculpted by its view of the refugee puzzle as a political matter, a viewpoint of its harsh encounter with the Vietnamese among other refugees.

CHAPTER 5

The Syria Dilemma

The Syrian civil conflict continued for over half a decade and the territorial advances made by Islamic State have resulted in the gravest refugee crisis dilemma in the world in years. Syrians are considered the second-largest refugee community globally. Following 2011, the disagreements between state and non-state actors have become stringent. The torrent of refugees has exhausted the supplies in the region and prompted xenophobia in nations throughout Europe. According to UNCHR, the Syrian war has destroyed a countless number of citizens and has uprooted millions.

PRC recognized Syria in the year 1946 and the diplomatic ties between both countries were instituted in 1956. During the Syrian civil war, China presented a comparatively low-profile position. After the conflict swelled, China has been wary and realistic about its strategy. China, unlike Russia that has not directly meddled in Syria by launching airstrikes has sought to maintain a safe hand from the dispute. The Chinese government has bickered that the West has bred the cataclysm in Syria, which has led to mass emigration making its purpose their responsibility. Li Guofu, a Middle East expert asserted that China was not a fitting destination for Middle Eastern refugees due to religious, cultural and political factors. Another Scholar Shen Jiru, of Chinese Academy of Social Sciences, stated that it was not appropriate to expect China to "clean up the mess" in Syria left by the US-led alliance.

In 2015, UNHCR in China declared that there were very few refugees and asylum seekers from Syria, Somalia, Nigeria, Iraq, and Liberia residing in China tentatively who were expecting to be shifted. China has not accepted a refugee resettlement policy that will assist to ease the refugee onerous hardship encountered by the other developing nations in the region inundated by the inrush. Also, the swelling Uighur dispute has made China reluctant to take in a huge number of Muslim refugees from the Middle East because China believes this could impede the country's identity politics and religious aspect. This common abhorrence of allowing refugees, particularly Muslims, primarily indicates China's growing "Islamophobia". Though Muslim ethnic groups such as Uyghur and Hui are only scarce percent of the whole Chinese population, the total percent of Chinese Muslims surpasses 20 million. Public polls reveal that an extensive bulk of Chinese firmly dislike the thought of settling Middle Eastern refugees, particularly Muslim refugees, inside China. There is a heavy insinuation of consternation amongst many Chinese nationals that China will be "Islamized". Professor Xi Wuyi from the Chinese Academy of Social Sciences had once stated "we are forced to give up our children to save space for foreigners." In this context, the Chinese tend to feel "deceived" by Communist Party of China (CPC) if it begins to accept Middle Eastern refugees. However, the CPC acknowledges the centrality of the Syrian region to its endurance, where former Chinese President Jiang Zemin travelled to the Arab League in 1996, and, in 2004, China sponsored the founding of the China-Arab States Cooperation Forum. Wang Yi, the foreign minister during his visit to Lebanon pronounced that, "To solve the refugee problems in the Middle East, we must first and foremost accelerate the political settlement of the Syria conflict," He further stated that "Refugees are not migrants" and as the circumstances change in Syria it is anticipated that the refugees will start to return to their homeland." Taking these statements into consideration, analysts called it animadversions and noted that China was not ready to change its stand on the refugee concern. At the occasion of the Geneva II peace conference in 2014, Wang Yi suggested five principles for promoting a political agreement that has underpinned China's official position such as the promotion of inclusive political transition, resolving the Syrian issue through political means, national reconciliation and unity to be accomplished, Humanitarian assistance in Syria and its neighboring nations and the future of Syria that must be decided by its people. Following President Xi Jinping's visit in 2016 to Syria, China stepped up its engagement in the conflict with the naming of Xie Xiaoyan, a diplomat, as China's first special envoy for the Syria dilemma.

China may be the only nation to consider performing the long-term and vast engagements to Syria's requirements. Syria is important to China for several reasons such as energy, economics, or security. For China, its Syria policy is primarily to maintain goodwill with the government and put itself in a robust position to negotiate beneficial terms for market entree or finance drives. China being one of the largest trading partners of Syria has made engagements to Syria for projects to the tune of $2 billion as it intends to fast track its rebuilding go. The World Bank reckons it could cost at least $250 billion to reconstruct Syria and China that aims to perform a significant function in the process and to maintain its presence by doing so. With over $3 trillion in foreign currency stocks, China has the ability to spend, finance and credit. Its goals through BRI present another strategic setting for it to consider a foremost position in Syria's reconstruction. For China's BRI aspirations, Lebanon and Syria serve as a path to the Mediterranean that is an alternative to the Suez Canal. China through massive stakes in anchorages in the easterly Mediterranean is endeavoring to revitalize important Eurasian trade corridors that connect China to Europe and further. China is working to be the center of international trade in the 21st centenary. The fusion of the port city of Tartus and Damascus into the BRI would add to China's economic status. The Chinese position in Iraq's rebuilding seemingly proposes the most reliable guide to its possible strategy in Syria. Lately, China is contemplating to enhance its sway in war-torn Syria and using the coronavirus pandemic to expedite these ideas. Huawei, a Chinese multinational technology company, has vouched to redevelop Syria's national telecoms network.

China's outlook that "Syria's freedom, sovereignty, autonomy and territorial uprightness must be considered and upheld," prompted China's Foreign Ministry to ask Turkey to "exercise caution" quickly after Turkey began "Operation Peace Spring", an armed intrusion in 2019 into north Syria. China has also been in adjustment with Russia on important matters associated with Syria, as demonstrated by its votes at the UNSC. China has donated $1 million to the World Health Organization (WHO), the World Food Program (WFP) and the International Committee of the Red Cross (ICRC) sequentially, for better food security and health assistance in Syria. But, China comprehending the fact that thousands of Uyghurs have moved to Syria to join the Islamic State and other terrorist outfits, is concerned about their return. Therefore, China believes that collaborating with Al-Assad regime could help if it is concerned about Uyghurs sliding back into China. It is also keen to neutralize this through renewed economic diplomacy to work on its reputation with the Muslim world after it has faced criticism with its engagement with the Uyghurs in Xinjiang. In November 2020, more sanctions were imposed on entities and individuals including parliament members who were supporting the Al-Assad during the civil war. As western sanctions continue to be imposed targeting Syria, China will feasibly be a more prominent global ally for Syria that can serve to counteract occidental influence. In June 2020, Syria in order to please its ally also became one of 53 nations to show its support for the Hong Kong national security law at the U.N.

Recently, as per the UNHCR, the economic distress due to COVID-19 pandemic has forced many thousands of Syrian refugees in the Middle East towards a despondent condition and has raised their humanitarian obligations. The number of helpless refugees who lack the necessary resources to remain in exile has drastically billowed due to public health urgency. Many refugees have likewise suffered from the spread of COVID, child labor, gender-based violence, loss of employment and insufficient wages, driving them to sever down on the most fundamental requirements such as food and medication. Though the majority of Syrian refugees in the region have been living below the poverty line (BPL), the pandemic has made it worse.

A more profound contemplation of Sino-Syrian bilateral ties is set to become critical to China's ambitious foreign policy in the post-COVID world and the Syrian government's idea for development and reconstruction. However, China has to equally play an important role concerning the Syrian refugees such as collaborating with UNHCR for "The Syria Refugee Response and Resilience Plan" and must farther enhance the protection of the most vulnerable refugees through assuring their subsistence. China, which is currying favor through its strategic interests and investments in Syria, must likewise focus on finding more possible solutions or strategies for the Syrian refugees.

CHAPTER 6

The Tibet Enigma

Tibet has been considered as a nonviolent and autonomous nation since ancient ages. As per the Rigveda and Atharvaveda, the ancient Indian holy texts, Tibet is called as "Trivistapa", the supernal abode, where "Mount Kailash" is known as the heart of the earth. During the 7th to the 9th century, Tibet was known to be the most stalwart military empires in Asia. After Buddhism spread to Tibet, the Tibetan people who were influenced by military got toned down, moving towards spiritual growth and advancement of peace and harmony. The country's armed power waned, and spiritual pursuance succeeded the impulse that led to an increase of nuns and monks.

Its major climacteric in history was when Tibet came under the rule of China in the year 1949. The Chinese call that Tibet remains to be an essential part of its territory is based on the chronicles of China where Tibet was under the Qing dynasty's rule from 1720 to 1912. However, after the dynasty was overthrown in 1911, Tibet moved to a new political era from 1912 to 1951. Post-1949, When Mao Zedong, the CCP chairman came to power in China and founded the PRC, he declared Tibet as a part of China and strenuously exerted its influence over Tibet under the pretense of "peaceful liberation," in 1951 by putting forth the 17-point deal. After Deng Xiaoping succeeded Mao Zedong, he recommended that the Tibet problem could be fixed if Tibetans stop attempting for severance from China. Zhou Enlai of China in 1955 vouched for Tibet and participated in the declaration pronouncing the "five principles of peaceful coexistence" amongst the countries in a conference held at Bandung, besides even agreeing with India regarding the state of Tibet in the year before but China hasn't been able to resolve the situation till date. After the illegal invasion of China, Tibet was inept of handling and carrying out its objectives and providing its inhabitants with protection and stability. "Tibetan government-in-exile" is a separatist political association trying to accomplish "Tibetan independence."

During the "1959 Tibet Uprising", His Holiness, Dalai Lama, the religious leader of Tibetans fled to India citing danger to his life. The Tibetans also resorted to arms to protect themselves. There was a sense of outrage and inability to the lamentations of the Tibetans throughout the world. The Tibet Uprising led to a prolonged ending-pitch of self-rule by the Tibetans where the communists took complete command over the land and the soul of the supernal abode, Tibet. When Dalai Lama and many other Tibetans fled to India, it was Jawaharlal Nehru, the first Prime Minister of independent India who came to their rescue. Nehru since 1959 displayed a keen engagement in the Tibetan refugee problems because of the fact that his China policy during the 1950s was harshly reprimanded in India where the critics sensed the Tibetan dilemma as the case of his policy collapse. Nehru attempted to put the Tibetan refugee predicament high on India's national agenda during the 1960s. Since the last four decades, Tibetans escaping Chinese oppression have tried and been given refuge in neighboring India and Nepal. Though India and the global community sympathized, they could not defend Tibet. However, Tibetans in India have essentially continued to remain stateless, continuing as "de facto" refugees. Tibetans likewise have fled in innumerable number to various countries. Their population in the U.S has risen significantly over the last decade. Tibetans who have fled have opted for the U.S citizenship and prompted to do so by the exile government as gaining a political voice in the U.S allowing them to be "ambassadors" for their lost home. The 1990 Immigration Act also opened the earliest large-scale migration of Tibetans to the U.S.

Though China asserts that Tibet is a domestic matter of China, it is apparent that Tibet has received worldwide media coverage and has become a global issue. Ranging from suppression of religious freedom, human rights abuses and illegal occupation of a nonviolent nation, the Tibetan struggle has been viewed as a source of inspiration by the world community to fight oppression and totalitarianism. Despite, the countries of Asia and Africa pronounced that imperialism could not have a spot in this contemporary world, China is reluctant to follow this and continues to exert its influence on its refugees like the Tibetans or the Uyghurs. The Tibetan culture and language are under big threat due to heightened state-sponsored Han Chinese migration toward the Tibetan regions.

The Tibetans are being relentlessly harassed by the Chinese and are continually being watched. Any kind of religion displayed by the people ends in unmerciful punishment. Dalai Lama, being the religious head of the Tibetans is helpless of even visiting Tibet in worry that the Chinese may detain him. Tibetans likewise are not even permitted to meet their spiritual head. Several monks and protestors have self-immolated in remonstrance of such stringent actions. Furthermore, Tashi Wangchuk, Tibetan language activist who stood up to defend the Tibetan language from Chinese dominance and influence was imprisoned for five years in 2018. On various happenings, people have been caught owning the photo of the Dalai Lama sometimes leading to confiscation of photo and further detention. Tibetan Buddhism is held as a threat and in addition to being strictly watched and the Buddhist monks are expelled and thrown out from temples. China has also announced a warning preventing the aged Tibetans and forbidding them from performing the Kora and other religious rituals. It is backbreaking for Tibetans to even own a passport. As per a Tibetan blogger, "Getting a passport is more difficult for a Tibetan than getting into heaven which is one of those 'preferential policies' given to us Tibetans by China's central government." China has likewise been using the "Hukou", a passport system that restricts access to public benefits depending on the person's place of birth.

China has drastically increased digital and human surveillance of Tibetans since last few years. Various social media sites have been banned in China where any kind of information can be scattered. Recently, Chinese hackers who had previously used an unknown iPhone security flaw to target ethnic minority Uighurs also went after Tibetans in exile as per some reports. Unfortunately, Tibetans in exile living in India have also been having a hard time after "We Chat" app was banned by Government of India along with various other Chinese apps following the 2020 India-China standoff. The following app was a lifeline for majority of the Tibetans to interact with their families and friends in Tibet.

China considers Tibet as critical to its strategic objectives. As China continues to grow more robust militarily, Tibetans might turn into a minority in China that could have a large impact on the Tibetan culture, religion and language in the coming years. The promises China had made to Tibet concerning their religious customs and their practices have been in hollow. Tibetans are bound to study Chinese in schools instead of the Tibetan language. CPC has been effectively working to obliterate any continuation of the Tibetan culture. It is teaching Tibetans new skills in order to make money and there has been huge scale resettlement that includes significant changes to social structures, culture and communities.

There has been a further "Sinification" of Buddhism. Many nuns and monks are also being compelled to attend "re-education" encampments. Furthermore, the movement of wanderers is entirely curbed where they are compelled to stay within houses than roam around areas as per their likings. The Chinese have imposed stern measures in case of any such movement. Tibetans have also been barred from singing their national anthem or displaying their national flag. China in the recent years has also frequently urged its next-door-neighbors and other nations to return Chinese refugees. Manifold tumults and revolts have erupted by the several Tibetans in the region to avert such a situation athwart the entire Tibet. This instability in the region has led to many economic catastrophes, family members being separated, destroying the properties and monasteries, suppression of religion, culture, right to maintain their own identity, Tibetans being used as forced labor and so on across the frontiers of Tibet. Assistant Secretary Robert Destro, a top US executive and newly appointed special adviser for Tibet matters in the State Department cited in 2020 that the "cancer" of "labor camps" in China had grown from Xinjiang to Tibet where many Tibetans are being driven into labor camps.

China does not allow any impediment from any other nation in its domestic matters and is attempting to reconstruct the values and mindsets of Tibetans to draw them into the country's contemporary mainstream, which involves pressing Tibet's devoted Buddhists to concentrate, less on religion and more on material expansion. For Chinese President Xi Jinping, the latchkey to dampen out calls for autonomy in Tibet and increasing CPC rule is producing economic advancement in one of China's most underdeveloped areas. The recent instance of economic progression was in Tibet's second-largest city, Shigatse, where low-income households have started to produce mushrooms, something that Tibetans haven't traditionally done earlier and then trading them to a state-supported organization. China in the coming years wants to annihilate poverty nationwide by putting forth poverty relief programmes. However, analysts state that China's attempts associating poverty eradication to a clutch of cultural life and the CPC's push to violate human rights for China's strategic ambitions. It has likewise presently taken the railway path to stiffen grip on Tibet by commencing the construction of Ya'an-Linzhi section of Sichuan-Tibet Railway nearby to India's border. In this context, Xi stated that China through the construction of the new railway path wants to safeguard national unity, strengthening stability in the frontier and increasing ethnic solidarity. From China's viewpoint, it further wants to exploit the enormous natural reserves in Tibet such as chromite and lithium that are abounding in the region where the new railway line traverses. China has funded massively in Tibet like building brand-new roads, housing, employment and access to re-education campaigns and healthcare to bring about a massive change to the region. The dark side of economic advancement in Tibet has resulted in enormous environmental harm through excess drilling, mining and closing of the rivers.

China despite being a fragment of the U.N and acknowledging various agreements and conventions including the Universal Declaration of Human Rights (UDHR), the Tibetans have been deprived of many fundamental human rights that have led to severe infringements of such agreements. China signed the three covenants in 1998 that constituted a section of the Bill of Rights. Nevertheless, they have not been approved yet. China has likewise unquestionably infringed the terms of the Geneva Convention, 1949, which prevents the transfer of a civilian population within a region that is already occupied. The Middle Way Approach (MWA) by His Holiness the Dalai Lama and the Central Tibetan Administration put forth to resolve the Tibet matter despite several rounds of Sino-Tibetan dialogues being conducted and a Memorandum on autonomy for the Tibetans were submitted to China in 2008, China did not acknowledge the MWA as it was against the Chinese constitution. MWA's significance is to bring about stability and co-existence within the Tibetan and Chinese people based on equality and mutual co-operation. Though this Chinese repression has often been reprobated by human rights organizations, there has been meager attentiveness proffered to the permissibility of such weight under international law. The 17-Point Agreement that was signed between the Central People's Government and the Local Government of Tibet on rules for the Peaceful Liberation of Tibet in affirming Chinese independence over Tibet continues to remain on the paper.

The office of the U.S Secretary of State, the U.S House of Representatives in the report 'The Elements of the China Challenge', published in 2020 announced the passing of bill declaring the importance of the support for autonomy for Tibetans in the PRC, and the work performed by the 14th Dalai Lama to foster global peace, equanimity, harmony and understanding, the U.S State Department has recently stated that Tibet is under Chinese military occupation. The House bill also beckons the Dalai Lama to address the US Congress to address peaceful resolutions to global conflicts. The bill further asked on the US government to back the Tibetan Policy and Support Act (TPSA) of 2002 and made the international community stand against CPC's hegemonic strategy. The new U.S administration under Joe Biden is expected to raise the weight of human rights and ideology in its China strategy concentrating on issues related to Xinjiang, Tibet and Hong Kong, which is crucial on the list to deal with China.

The Canadian and Swiss ambassadors to China in 2020 made a rare visit to Tibet to witness local situations and growing problems with their Chinese hosts but have been quiet to a great extent about the situation in the region. Switzerland has been one of the earliest nations to grant refuge to Tibetans escaping China's ruthless occupation of Tibet. Switzerland has likewise been a champion of discussion between China and the representatives of His Holiness the Dalai Lama. The Tibet Bureau Geneva has embraced Switzerland's motility to incorporate the improvement of human rights as an instrumental segment of the political discussion and for advancing the human rights condition in Tibet problem. The bureau has likewise said Switzerland should take a more active stand on Tibet and include the affairs of Tibetans and Uyghurs in its Foreign Policy Strategy regarding China 2021-24. Switzerland has tabled its matters about the absence of respect for human rights in China, particularly the mode of treatment of Tibetans by the Chinese officials. Lately, there have been reports of incidence of surveillance and censorship on Tibetans residing in Switzerland, Sweden and New York by Chinese officials.

Tibet remains to be an autonomous state and has not lost its statehood as per the International Law. However, even if the state of Tibet as an autonomous state and an occupied territory of China is still to be settled due to reasons that though it is deemed independent being a part of China. If China is determined and inclined to safeguard national sovereignty and territorial uprightness, it should likewise try to respect the cultural and political sentiments of the Tibetans. A self-governing Tibet can also assure peace and tranquility at the Line of Actual Control (LAC).

CHAPTER 7

The Invisible Refugees of North Korea

North Korean defector routes

Photo Courtesy: Www.wikimediacommons.com

The relationship between China and North Korea has often been described as a special one with regard to historic, cultural and ideological affinity. China has exercised power in the Korean peninsula historically and has watched the neighborhood against intrusions. Both the countries have buttressed cooperative relations. North Korea has been geopolitically crucial for China due to the outset of the Cold War, the founding of PRC and the helpful government of China in Korea, it became pre-eminent to serve as a shield territory against occidental governments and mainly capitalism. China also backed North Korea throughout the Korean War. Following the Korean War, when North Korea started its development plans, China's help has been important for their bilateral ties. Also, China has considerable economic links with North Korea. Between 2000 and 2015, as per the Korea Trade-Investment Promotion Agency, the mutual trade has progressed over time. Despite the advent of more robust sanctions and the fissionable tests and rocket launches, North Korea is nevertheless clinging on to China for trade and financial purposes. China has remained requisite for North Korea concerning defence, finance and development.

However, It is seen that China has been following a consistent policy of repatriation towards North Koreans people who cross the border into China. According to the Chinese government, North Koreans who flee their country are not treated as refugees because of the fact that they tend to escape due to economic reasons who cannot be defined as refugees as per the U.N convention which defines, "A refugee is someone who has been forced to flee his or her country because of persecution, war, or violence".

North Koreans people have been fleeing to China through the northeastern provinces of Jilin, Heilongjiang, and Liaoning and both countries have taken measures to tighten border security. It is estimated that 200,000 North Koreans are hiding in China making them the largest population outside of North Korea according to 2012 statistics. As per the Human Rights Watch (HRW) reports, refugees who are returned to North Korea after being captured were sent to labor encampments and disgraced as "traitors" to the North Korean regime. These refugees have been fleeing to China since 1983, with drastic increase following North Korea's famine in the mid-1990s. Exile and trial also extend to the refugee's family. It is believed that these refugees are not typically considered to be members of the ethnic Korean community and the Chinese census does not take this into consideration much. Some North Korean refugees who are unable to obtain transport to South Korea marry ethnic Koreans in China and settle there. They tend to blend into the community but are subject to deportation if discovered by the authorities. It is observed that women are particularly vulnerable to violence such as prostitution, rape, arranged marriages and bride traffickers. Border issues like extortion, human smuggling, poverty, food security and trafficking, exploitation are another set of growing problems. WFP has stated that food security continues to be a daily struggle for majority of North Koreans. The people who defected from North Korea were deceived into China as cybersex drudges. More fixed relations with China beckons a piece of unfavorable headlines for escapees. China likewise doesn't permit North Koreans to apply for political asylum. China and South Korea are parties to the 1951 Refugee Convention and 1967 Protocol whereas North Korea is not a party to either instrument. Despite this, China has violated the International law and its obligations to follow the principle of non-refoulement under the UN refugee convention.

During 1960s, China and North Korea had signed a secret agreement to govern security in the border area and the collapse of the Soviet Union during the cold war made China to find ways to maintain its interests in a unipolar, U.S dominated international system. Hence, China began to normalize diplomatic relations with South Korea in 1992 and because of this North Korea accused China publicly. But when North Korea faced its greatest famine, China used this as an opportunity to maintain its influence in North Korea by providing financial assistance. Ever since the North Korean famine during the 1990's, many have traversed the border. North Koreans flee their homeland due to factors such as poverty, the hardcore authoritarian regime, food shortages and human rights violations. Citizens who flee into Dandong, a Chinese province are sent back to North Korea by the Chinese government.

North Korea has been one of the most repressive authoritarian countries in the world, which has been ruled for seven decades by the Worker's Party of Korea (WPK). The constitution describes North Korea as "a dictatorship of people's democracy" under the authority of the WPK that has been given constitutional supremacy over other political parties. The WPK is the ruling political party of North Korea, which has been in power following its conception in the year 1948. North Korea follows a strict visa and travel policy. North Korean nationals normally cannot easily travel throughout the country and to other foreign countries. Immigration and Emigration are stringent as the government of North Korea treats emigrants from the nation as defectors. People who are thought to bring benefit to the country by foreign travel like the athletes and artists are the only ones who are granted exit visas.

China despite being a party to the Refugee Convention and Protocol, has not allowed U.N. agencies and the UNHCR to have access to North Koreans who are living in China since it considers these individuals as economic migrants who traverse the borders mainly due to need of food. But in most of the high profile asylum cases, China permits the North Koreans to travel to a third country and later move to Seoul, South Korea.

South Korea provides citizenship along with financial aid and is considered to be the major destination for North Korean refugees. UNHCR office in Seoul helps the refugees in resettlement programs. China prefers to negotiate a proper dialogue through quiet diplomacy with North Korea. Nevertheless, as per the critics the main reason majority of North Koreans are trying to escape is because of the hardcore political rule of the regime in Pyongyang. During the famine and the Cultural Revolution in China during the 1960's, many Chinese people sought refuge in North Korea. But the situation was reversed ever since 1990's. Keeping this in mind the Chinese authorities should remember the hospitality their fellow citizens received in North Korea and treat desperate people who fled, with dignity and respect.

Since North Korea has been a closed country with no access to Internet and proper employment, people tend to lack knowledge and skills in the outside world so because of this fact an estimated one million North Koreans live in South Korea after escaping the Pyongyang regime. In the Seoul-based South Korea Hana Foundation the refugees tend to get their first exposure to southern customs like Internet and employment and additionally have access to various programmes that exist in the Church jurisdiction for people who want to enter society in a dignified way. However, the number of those making successful escapes to South Korea, via China has steadily declined over the past few years. This can also mean that there may be a positive viewpoint in the relationship between the fall in numbers and the peace efforts where some North Koreans still hope that the life in the country would improve. Recently, South Korea's government and North Korean defectors have locked horns against each other once again. Many defector groups in South Korea published in June 2020 that they would advance to send pamphlets to North Korea that are designed to communicate news about the external world and criticize North Korea's human rights violations and nuclear ambitions. The following pamphlets are considered by North Korea as an attack on its government. Also, human rights advocates and defector groups have sent such pamphlets to North Korea using balloons for years. Due to the pamphlets issue, the Seoul government has proposed to expedite fresh laws to prevent pamphlet protests. Also, there have been growing concerns over the government's biased stance toward North Korean defectors after Moon Jae-in administration came to power. Moon Jae-in in 2019 has pledged to achieve unification of the Korean peninsula by 2045 that will also mark the 100th anniversary of liberation. He likewise has plans to jointly host the 2032 Seoul-Pyongyang Olympics. South Korea should also recognize the genuine partnership of North Korea and the intellectual resources they have. As per the South Korean constitution, North Koreans are considered as citizens of the Republic of Korea and hence have the right to be resettled there. Jobs, benefits and also education programs should be provided to the North Korean refugees. Non Government Organizations (NGO's) can play a huge role in this process too.

Post COVID pandemic, the North Korea defections have been at record low. The fall in the number of North Koreans escaping came after Kim's government moved quickly to isolate the country due to the deteriorating condition in China. It led to the sudden closure in the land, air and sea routes in North Korea in January 2020. North Korea, with a weak and ill-equipped healthcare system, has not reported a single COVID case till date and has sealed its frontiers to halt the spread of the virus into its region. As North Korea has been facing an economic disaster due to negative economic drifts and global sanctions caused by the pandemic, this situation has further led to several refugees attempting to traverse Thailand's presently tightly-closed land and river borders which is anticipated by certain observers to spring up in the coming times. Due to the intensified security situation, it is highly uncertain as to how many North Korean refugees will be able to make it through the journey.

CHAPTER 8

Xinjiang on the Big Plate – "Sinicisation" of Islam

Whether in Xinjiang or anywhere else in the world, refugees are oftentimes the prey of diplomatic and geopolitics calculation by nation-states. China is meeting increasing worldwide criticism over its handling of Uighurs. The Xinjiang Dispute is a separatist dispute in Xinjiang whose southern region is known as East Turkestan and northern region is known as Dzungaria. The Uyghurs are a Muslim, Turkic-language speaking ethnic community found throughout Central-Asia. The range of Xinjiang wars that took place throughout the beginning and middle of the 20th Century presented an important function in the East Turkestan Liberation Movement (ETLM). The region is recognized to be possessing many nuclear testing sites and also overflowing in natural reserves such as oil, Jade, copper, coal, gold, natural gas etc., that are strategically important as it shares international frontiers with Pakistan, Kyrgyzstan, Afghanistan, Tajikistan, Russia, Mongolia, Kazakhstan and India controlled Kashmir. Xinjiang has prospered adequately in comparison to other regions in China although it also hosts the largest rural-urban gap in terms of a capital gap where bulk of the country's poverty-stricken live on the countryside. Xinjiang is fundamental to China's strategic importance as it additionally holds crucial significance for China's projected energy demands.

The Xinjiang area was captured by the Chinese Qing dynasty in the 18th century and Xinjiang was formally consolidated as a Chinese region in 1884, which also was when the Qing dynasty began calling Xinjiang as a new frontier. Following the Dungan Revolt (1862–77), the region was renamed as Xinjiang in 1884, which is presently a part of the PRC, notwithstanding the resistance of the local community. However, Uyghur separatists allege that the province wasn't a part of Mainland China and was illegally fused into the PRC in 1949 and has since remained under Chinese control. China in the 1950s started a program of mass migration of ethnic Han Chinese into Xinjiang, thereby enhancing local hostility to Chinese rule.

The large majority of Uighurs' live in Xinjiang. Uyghur nationalists claim that 5 per cent of Xinjiang's community in 1949 was Han and 95 per cent was Uyghur and that in 1800 during the Qing dynasty the Han was about one-third of Xinjiang's population. Although the Uyghurs historically were the majority in the region, ethnic Chinese presently constitute more than half of the population of Xinjiang and hold the majority of administrative and government jobs. Some of the province's central cities such as Urumqi, Hotan, and Kashgar have been strategically significant stations on the Silk Road, the legendary trade route that connected China, the Middle East, and Europe for ages. But the region's chronicle is more complex. In 1949, separatists succinctly proclaimed autonomy for "East Turkestan", the Uyghur name for Xinjiang. Although it didn't last long China took charge quickly after the establishment of the communist state that same year, where the vision of self-governance and intrusion lives on. Separatism under Communist government started during the Maoist era where Xinjiang was subjected to extreme periods of uncertainty that associated with the fluctuating state policies of the "Great Leap Forward" and "Cultural Revolution". CPC rebukes the fury on Islamist militants and separatists from the Uyghur community who want to set up an autonomous state named East Turkestan. Separation in Xinjiang has been produced in part by China's handling of the Uyghurs due to religious concerns. The presence of Islam in the region can be sketched back to the 8th century. In the 11th century, Mongols from the east invaded Central Asia and conquered the Turks, a reason why many Turkish-speaking Chinese today descend from Mongol and Turkish tribal families. After the concluding period of the Cultural Revolution and Deng Xiaoping's taking over control of China, the policy of "Reform and Open-up" was adopted by the government, which drastically altered the economic arrangement in China. Xinjiang was no exception.

After the September 9/11 attack in the U.S, China grabbed the opportunity to reframe its conflict with the Uyghurs as a dimension of the global war against terrorism. The state felt the need to shield its frontiers from a penetration of more coercive forms of Islam from Afghanistan, Pakistan, Tajikistan, Kyrgyzstan and Kazakhstan. Uyghurs initially came to global notice when the U.S and its allies attacked Afghanistan in 2001. While advancing their association with the Taliban under the flag of the ETIM, the Uyghur jihadists have now expanded to the Middle East and Southeast Asia. The CPC's trammel in Xinjiang has swept an approximated one million ethnic Uyghurs and other principally Muslim minorities into "vocational education centers'" that diverse studies and reports have revealed as rigid internment camps. The amount of Uighurs seeking refuge has been on the surge abroad, with Uyghurs outside China bearing the great likelihood of detention. There are instances where some Uyghurs fled to other countries on student visas especially to France, Hungary, and the Nordic countries, to never return. Although the Bush administration originally was loath to equate its fight against terrorism with domestic crackdowns on Uyghur separatists, the State Department of the U.S added the ETIM in 2002 to its "Terrorist watch list". The ETIM has been accused by the U.S State Department on its responsibility in various acts of terrorism in China like incendiarism attacks, assassinations, shelling of cinemas, buses, markets and hotels and it was further accused of having nexus with the Al Qaeda's terrorist network. The U.N on the first anniversary of the 9/11 attack named the ETIM as a backer of terrorism. China blamed Xinjiang in a separate report to the U.N that ETIM factions were operating in Chechnya, Uzbekistan, Tajikistan and Kyrgyzstan.

China likewise announced its first ever "terrorist list" which included the Eastern Turkistan Liberation Organization (ETLO), World Uighur Youth Congress (WUYC), and the East Turkistan Information Centre (ETIC). The CPC is conscious that conferring the Uyghurs greater independence would impel dissidents such as in Tibet or Taiwan. The most deciding issue one needs to understand is the Chinese states elimination of Cultural and religious freedom. In the past ethnic leaders like Kadeer allege that the Chinese regime is trying to wipe out the Uyghur culture and language and has secretly executed thousands of Uyghurs. China sought to describe Uyghur separatism as another face of the global terrorism peril that the world community must confront in the beginning of 2000s pitting "modern" countries such as the U.S and China against non-state Islamic foes.

In the Khunjerab Pass border in Northwest Xinjiang Region, crooks and terrorists attempt to smuggle drugs or guns into China. Khunjerab pass is more near Afghanistan and Tajikistan. Ever since the Khunjerab Pass crossing opened in 1982, drug dealers have been attempting to take benefit of Xinjiang to get their profitable stock onto the Chinese market. The drugs are normally grown and manufactured in Afghanistan and are then transported to northern Pakistan, where the majority of stock is packaged into smaller bags before being smuggled into China. "Guns and drugs" always go hand in hand. In the Khunjerab Pass border in Northwest Xinjiang Region, crooks and terrorists attempt to smuggle drugs or guns into China. Khunjerab pass is more near Afghanistan and Tajikistan. The Khunjerab Pass in Kashgar Prefecture has a vital place in law enforcement in terror-plagued southern Xinjiang. Drugs likewise came from the "Golden Crescent," a region that extends from Afghanistan to Iran via Pakistan, where the large bulk of the world's illicit opium is grown in the three countries mountainous peripheries. The issue is not only about drugs, people living on the Xinjiang region are accustomed to the catchword "using drugs to foster terrorism". It is assumed that many rifle shops exist along the Khunjerab Pass to Gilgit where people can own a wide range of guns if they obtain an easily obtained license. It is also more accessible to obtain a gun without permission in Afghanistan. The Khunjerab Pass in Kashgar Prefecture has a vital place in law enforcement in terror-plagued southern Xinjiang. Drugs likewise came from the "Golden Crescent," a region that extends from Afghanistan to Iran via Pakistan, where the large bulk of the world's illicit opium is grown in the three countries' mountainous peripheries.

Following the 1990s China has attempted to normalize associations with the Central Asian countries by resolving border disputes specifically, pragmatically connected to Uyghur separatism. Uyghurs in Central Asia can be divided into two groups, which is the mainly secular, Russified long-term residents from Europe who are not preoccupied with the Xinjiang issue and the recent arrivals from China. Chinese are concerned about the Uyghur diaspora in Central Asia, who have created, urged politicians and have employed the Internet to publicize Central Asian Republics efficiently their complaints to a global audience. Following the late 1990s, the CPC appears to have employed a carrot and stick artifice in Xinjiang, granting financial advantages to the Uyghurs that have decayed their aspirations for freedom and autonomy while callously pressing down on the province.

In 1994 Chinese Premier, Li Peng visited Central Asia ensuring financial support to the struggling governments in return for promises that they would not shelter Uyghur activists. The subsequent year both the nations signed an accord under which Kazakh security services would watch Uyghur activities and share their findings with China. In 1996, the CPC government ordered "Strike Hard" campaigns or government operations intended to fight crimes and any perils to stability by accelerating detentions, prosecutions and sentencing convicts. Even after Xinjiang was regarded as China's "Wild West", China would seldom report illegal separatist activity, ethnic riots, or the detentions of the Uyghur activists from the beginning of 1980s to 1997.

Central Asia's 500,000 strong Uyghur Diasporas, 25% of Uzbekistan's 27 million residents enjoy proximal blood relations with the Uyghurs where China deems it to be a twisted actuality. Some global anxieties persist concerning the return extraditions to China of the known Uyghur separatists from states such as Uzbekistan, Kazakhstan, and Kyrgyzstan to face death penalties. China is concerned that Uyghurs in Central Asia will sympathize with those in Xinjiang and grant support and refugee with Uyghurs being the seventh-largest minority in Kazakhstan where they enjoy certain political and cultural independence. Kyrgyzstan has made numerous shots to break down on Uyghurs on their soil. The chief purpose that some Uyghurs have radicalized is because of perceived repression by the Chinese state. Historically, China had predicaments uniting culturally and politically its ethnic Muslim community in Xinjiang, and this national problem has influenced China's relationships with the neighboring countries of Central Asia. China's presence in Central Asia has increased in contemporary times, and it has become substantial across the imperative, political, and economic panorama of the region. Some reports assert that there is a presence of Chinese military vehicles identified as Dong Feng EQ 2050 which is the equivalent of American Mine Resistant Ambush Protected Vehicle, Humvee, inside a Central Asian region called "Little Pamir", an arid tableland close to the frontier. In 2017, CPC had declared that it will shortly use drones, fit barbed wire fencing and surveillance cameras to guard the 5,600-kilometre border of its Muslim-majority Xinjiang region adjoining Pakistan controlled Kashmir and Afghanistan.

In the mid-1990s China pushed for the alteration of "Shanghai Five" regional conference into the Shanghai Cooperation Organization (SCO) founded in 2001. China's mounting anxieties about the separatist and the militant action led Beijing to push the SCO to focus on the trans-border menaces such as the Islamic extremism, radicalism and drug trafficking. The Regional Anti-Terrorist Structure (RATS) was founded in 2002, which is multilateral security collaboration between SCO member states. In the year 2003 and 2006 China has carried armed exercises with SCO members, concentrate on frontier security and strikes on mock terrorist training camps to create state assistance for cracking down on Uyghur separatists. The suppression of Muslim Uyghurs has long motivated fighters from Central Asia to assist them. Based on the "Cooperation Program to Combat Terrorism, Separatism and Extremism in 2013-2015", RATS set up a cyber specialist group in 2013 to enhance the pragmatic collaboration of the SCO member countries in the battle against online activities of extremism, terrorism, separatism. In May 2014, China launched its "Strike Hard Campaign against the Uyghurs. To heighten the mutual trust and increase the law enforcement association in the area of cyber counter-terrorism further, the RATS Council passed the Resolution No. 386. SCO was originally set up to counter "international jihadists" from inciting fury in the Xinjiang province, and has served to secure assurances from Central Asian powers that they will never assist "militant separatists" based on religious and ethnic commonalities. One can fairly presuppose that Central Asia has become even more vital to the protection of China.

China needs to uncover an alternative solution or adapt to regulations to strengthen the protection of civil liberties in its counter-terrorism activities. Besides these traditional anti-terror mechanisms, relevant officials of member countries of the SCO collectively hosted the Xiamen 2015 online counter-terrorism exercise. It was successfully held on October 14, 2015 in the southeastern Chinese coastal city of Xiamen, Fujian province. This is the first joint online exercise to counter terrorists hosted by the SCO. Though China usually avoids domestic interference, it has used the SCO to pressurize the governments of Kazakhstan and Kyrgyzstan to close down Uyghur political parties and newspapers. China also hosted the largest army exercise with SCO members after 2004 within its frontiers. It has also been working with its Central Asian member countries through intelligence, facilities and resource sharing in substantial portion for counter-terrorism missions. Nations in Central Asia are likewise in vast need of security and safety, which gives the states of the province and China common ground in dealing with the "international jihadists". China asserts that crisis in Xinjiang would lead to a deterioration in external oil investment risk infrastructure development and reduce other kinds of international investment. Many Central Asian nations have also used 'Uyghur Card" to curry favor with China. In 2003, China created its version of a terrorism surveillance list.

Beijing maintains that Xinjiang has always been part of China. Some safeguard actions that China has implemented cover the interference of the People's Liberation Army (PLA) and numerous paramilitary organizations like the Xinjiang Production and Construction Corps (XPCC) and People's Armed Police (PAP). China's first comprehensive anti-terrorism bill, passed at the end of 2015, took effect on the first day of 2016. China's growing crackdown in the region may generate both a fresh breaker in Uyghur radicalization and a new puddle of recruits ready to join in jihadist movements overseas.

The suppression of the movement in Xinjiang for protection of the basic rights to defend its religious and cultural independence and identities requires far more comprehensive attention by the international community. China has been tracking Uyghurs for using a mobile app. Detailed Chinese government reports unveil how Chinese officials have been targeting users of the "Zapya" app developed by a Chinese startup that assists users to download the Quran and share spiritual education with near and dear ones as part of their crackdown against the Muslim Uyghur community. The Uyghur activists state that many families have disappeared into the detention camps, or have been killed. As per media reports, Uyghurs were detained after they were found using the "We Chat" app to educate about Islam. However, China has frequently disavowed involvement in cyber attacks or any violation of the Uyghurs. According to Darren Byler, an anthropologist at the University of Washington who researches about the Uyghurs asserted that, "The Internet gave space for religious and cultural expression, but then later it became evidence of their religious extremism". The Uyghur community has been particularly targeted after CPC leader Chen Quanguo became Xinjiang's party secretary in 2016. Under his authority, a large surveillance base was unfurled across the province created to observe and regulate the population. The "Sinicisation of Islam" in Xinjiang province has intensified greatly.

IO's like HRW and Amnesty International allege that 'cultural oppression' of the Uyghurs is the problem of ethnic protests in Xinjiang. China reacted to the swelling turmoil in the region in various forms. The realignment of Central Asian policies concerning Uyghurs can be observed to expand over the years due to conflicts between 1997-2000 which were quickly put down by regional states. Since 2000 the ethnic strains have worsened among the Uyghurs and the Han Chinese. Muslims in Xinjiang claim the government's tactics in its intervention in religious worship and deliberate operations against Uyghur culture. Like the other Muslim minorities in China, the Uyghurs in Xinjiang witnessed their religious texts and mosques razed, their spiritual leaders persecuted and individual followers imprisoned. After Mao, the government lifted several of the restrictions as part of its effects to enact amelioration strategies and liberalization. The enhanced medical care, decreasing infant-mortality rate, and laxity in China's "One-child policy" helped Xinjiang's community swelling in the past. But, China is lately forcing birth control in Xinjiang to crush the Uyghur community. After the founding of the Soviet Union, several urban Uyghurs seldom chose Russian names for their babies in cities like Urumqi. But since last decades, Uyghurs began giving Muslim names to their babies such as Muhammad', 'Arafat' and 'Jihad' in Xinjiang that has been largely disliked and objected by CPC. In 2015, Chinese authorities put a prohibition on beards for Muslim men and veils for Muslim women in public spaces and likewise ban on fasting in the holy month of Ramadan, and directed Muslim-owned eateries to remain open during the Ramadan period.

"Ethnic Cleansing" has been drastically intensifying in Xinjiang with such terrible incidents.

HRW said that approximately 13 million Muslims in Xinjiang have been reduced to group punishment, restrictions on movement, increased religious constraints, forced political indoctrination and communications, mass monitoring and surveillance in breach of international human rights law. The CPC has even branded Islam an "Ideological Illness" and has damaged many mosques in the province. In the encampments, Uyghur detainees are required to study and glorify the ruling CPC, Chinese Mandarin and suffer repeated psychological vituperations and physical injuries. It is also reported that thousands of college educated Uyghur youths have a challenge obtaining employment while Han graduates manage to obtain jobs in the government sector. The educated Uyghurs are assigned to the lower ranks in their work due to their ethnicity. The further increased economic marginalization of the Uyghurs has turned them to substance abuse, prostitution and sexually transmitted diseases.

In particular, China expects to avoid Xinjiang residents coming into contact with the global world to increase awareness of their situation, and for Uyghurs who have been educated abroad, China may hope to crack down on Uyghur intellectuals who may become hotbeds of revolution. China's attempt to construct a labyrinth of sources has also seeded scepticism and animosity within Uyghur communities overseas. The seriousness of the situation can be seen from the major events of Uyghur terrorism: In February 1992, two buses exploded in Urumqi, resulting in at least 3 deaths, and 23 injured and reports stated that the attacks were perpetrated by the ETIM. In June 2012, Chinese official media reported that 6 men attempted to hijack Tianjin Airlines flight GS7554 from Hotan to Urumqi, Xinjiang. In April 2013 Xinjiang ethnic clashes killed 21 people including 15 police officers. In October 2013 Tiananmen Square attack, a fiery car blaze killed 5 and injured dozens. In September 2015, an unidentified man attacked off-duty workers at a coalmine, killing 50, among them 5 police officers in Xinjiang. These events raise doubts on how the terrorists are procuring weapons to carry out the atrocities.

The Trump administration blamed China of running "Concentration camps" and subsequently called its operations in Xinjiang the "stain of the century." However, the CPC regards these attacks as associated both to global jihadist movements and the Xinjiang freedom or independence. Police are with "fists and daggers" in the battle against terrorism as per Xi Jinping who was on a tour to the western Xinjiang region where officials say members of a Muslim minority are waging a fierce separatist drive. The Islamic State leader Abu Bakr al-Baghdadi's threat to occupy part of Xinjiang and his message to the Uyghurs that "Your brothers all over the world are waiting for your rescue and are anticipating your brigades" appears to have been taken seriously by China. Uyghur refugees have caused heat in China with the Uyghur "liberation army" hired from pro-Soviet émigrés. Many Uyghurs according to Chinese authorities have joined the Islamic State to fight in Syria. However, it is understood that the aims and purposes of Uyghurs are not compatible with those of Islamic jihadist organizations. The Uyghur separatists are triggered not by religious dogma or ideological fervor but by nationalistic and separatist movements. It has never been adequately illustrated that a substantive organizational connection between al Qaeda and the ETIM exists. Therefore it is challenging to draw any clear-cut consequence about relations within the two organizations. There are numerous other causes the Uyghurs are cutout with the Chinese authorities. For instance, Uyghurs are frustrated with the widespread corruption by the Chinese government. Numerous Uyghurs protest that they are denied economic opportunities due to an inrush of Han Chinese into the region. In 2004, hundreds of Uyghur residents demurred government policies to shove them off their farmlands without adequate compensation to construct a dam. "Human Security theory" as applied by Clarke (Griffith University, Brisbane) presents a more reliable lens through which to observe China's handling of the Uyghurs.

Concerning the BRI, the "Silk Road Fund" will possibly reinforce Xinjiang's position in China's economic cooperation with its energy-rich neighbors and be a blessing to the livelihood of the Uyghurs is an added solution to crackdown on crisis in the region. As China's investment and trade along the "New Silk Road", advances to expand, the province may become economically dependent upon Beijing. By developing extensive gas and oil pipelines and a system of transportation links, China is making itself economically requisite to Xinjiang and the nations lying in the modern-day Silk Road. By reducing other significant competitors, Central Asian nations do not have many other partners to turn to who can offer few of the benefits of working with China. Their investment and diplomacy and also the hands-off strategy to politics make the Chinese the perfect match for authoritarian governments in Central Asia. This would make for a win-win situation because Chinese trade partners in Central Asia will likely take the same hands-off approach to China's domestic strategy towards the Uyghurs. On the whole, China seems to be successfully gaining on the economic opportunities within the region while increasing the isolation of the Uyghurs. President Xi declared that 'long term security of the independent region is important to the whole country's reform, development and stability, as well as to national unity, ethnic harmony and national security'. But despite China's online censorship, research has found that social media presents opportunity for the Chinese Muslims to communicate with the external members.

China has lately been involved in increased global cooperation to prevent Uyghur communities to relocating to other countries. Recently, Turkey has warned to extradite Uyghur refugees to China, where they could face arrest after Turkish officials denied their requests for long-term residency and refuge status. Turkey that was a haven historically for Uyghurs has turned against the refugees and is looking for greater involvement in the BRI. Turkey angered China by showing concern about reports of restrictions on Uyghurs worshipping and fasting during Ramadan. The Turkish protesters have also marched on China's embassy and consulate in Turkey over the treatment of Uyghurs. Many Muslim majority nations have also been quiet on ethnic oppression of Uyghurs to not provoke China militarily, diplomatically and economically. Approximately half of the signatories were Muslim-majority countries, such as Qatar, Syria, Pakistan, the United Arab Emirates (UAE), and Saudi Arabia, as per to the CPC. Also, many nations do not hold the best human rights records and therefore show minimal interest in raising a red flag in the ongoing problems of China. Kazakhstan has also recently refused to offer asylum to Uyghurs fearing China, a deadly and ruthless next-door-neighbor. As per China's directions, even Pakistan has started armed operations to clear out the ETIM training posts in its tribal regions. Uyghurs who have fled the turmoil in Xinjiang have traveled clandestinely through Southeast Asia to Turkey. Some of the Uyghur students who moved abroad for higher studies have been asked by China to become spies in the last decade.

On the bright side, few Asian nations and institutions are willing to offer refugee for Uyghurs such as the case of Malaysia endangering the vengeance of China. The U.K government in September 2020 held proposals placed by members of parliament to permit Uyghurs and other Muslim minorities to register a petition in the high court against the genocide-taking place in Xinjiang. British lawmakers have called for sanctions over Uyghur human rights abuses. The European Court of Human Rights (ECHR) had directed Bulgaria to pause its deportation of some Uyghur refugees because they could be lacerated or killed by the Chinese officials. Chinese do not want Uyghurs to secure the type of universal sympathy held by Tibetans, another oppressed ethnic community in China. As per the Bulgarian Ministry of Foreign Affairs reports, constraints were put on the observance of religious holidays, the passports of the Uyghurs were taken and Islamic writing and literature was forbidden. Uyghur refugees are not able to campaign openly in different parts of Europe due to shakedown, monitoring and coercion by China. Despite years of oppression of Uyghurs, westward nations are now recognizing the scale of the campaign of mass incarceration that China is inflicting in Xinjiang that has caused deportations. The U.S has continued backdoor arrangements to resettle some Uyghur refugees in other nations alternatively, like in Bermuda. However, the U.S is reluctant to accept Uyghur refugees as they are facing increasing issues of surveillance from China.

China should work more towards strengthening its connection and understanding about the Uyghur area and also the consequences of policies in Xinjiang. Unless the culture, language, religion, education, and work of the Uyghur community are preserved and respected, Xinjiang will remain to be stained with blood and violence. Supporting the idea of a stable and secure Xinjiang rather destabilizing the region will be indispensable to shielding these interests.

CHAPTER 9

The Slow Asphyxiation of the Kachins

Ethnic battles have risen as one of the most challenging problems in Myanmar's continuing political shift. China has continued to be in hush on the Kachin row despite its frontier being at the corner of the cannon bullets shedding. China and Burma in 1954, established bilateral ties through a collective announcement that declared the Five Principles of Peaceful Coexistence that came to be known as China's "peaceful rise". Following 1947, consecutive governments in Burma have shared great ties with China. Though China has mostly followed a strategy of "non-interference" in domestic matters of another nation, its operations in the Kachin conflict represent a shift in this situation. But post-1962 armed coup, Burma-China ties degenerated. China readily rendered material assistance to the Communist Party of Burma (CPB) and Kachin Independence Army (KIA) in their armed strifes against the military regime of Burma. After the stringent anti-Chinese tumults in Rangoon, bilateral ties acidulated more in 1967 and Chinese assistance for the CPB intensified. In the contemporary times, China has been a sturdy political confederate of Myanmar military regime, exercising or threatening its veto power at the UNSC to halt or prevent U.N resolutions that can lead to global action in response to the Myanmar human rights issues.

Historically, The Kachins are a group of different tribes with similar languages and cultural compositions also known as the "Jingpo" people in China. They are a confederation of ethnic groups who dwell the Kachin Hills in northern Myanmar's Kachin and the nearby Yunnan in China and few parts of Northeastern India. The Kachin ancestors are said to have originated on the Tibetan Plateau, and relocated south, reaching Myanmar apparently in the 1400s or 1500s CE. Anthropologists note that the Kachin people are quite recognized for diverse abilities or traits. They are known to be very disciplined warriors, a point that the British colonial government took benefit of when it hired massive numbers of Kachin people into the colonial militia. Kachin area is abundant in natural reserves consisting of tropical timber, gold, and jade. The Kachins have a deep understanding of essential skills such as forest survival and herbal healing by utilizing local plant items apart from having very tangled associations with the various groups and tribes in the ethnic group, and also for their talent as artists.

Both the Kachins in Burma and Jingpo belong to the same ethnic group and any hard stratagems against the Kachins by China might aggravate the Jingpo group in Yunnan area driving to an internal security fulmination in Yunnan.

When Burma attained its freedom in 1948, the Kachins got its state with the support that they would be granted regional independence. But the Myanmar central government proved to be more interventionist than it had agreed. The government infringed in Kachin matters, while further stripping the province of community funds and leaving it adhering on raw supplies stock for its significant income or revenue. Frustrated with the way matters were going out of control, at the beginning of 1960s, combative Kachin leaders bred the KIA and began a guerrilla war upon the government. In the U.N, China provided the strongest diplomatic support to Myanmar and protected it from relentless action from the UNSC to woo the Myanmar government with amity. The fury between the Myanmar government military and the KIA has led to fury and civil uncertainty in Myanmar. This friction took place following the Independence of Myanmar from the British. People from Burma including ethnic Kachins, have escaped to Yunnan province to avoid the armed conflict for decades. By 1994 when a ceasefire deal was acknowledged between KIA and the Burmese government, an approximated 20,000 Kachins fled into China. As the uprooted Kachins remain to live in dreadful situations, human rights groups are calling on China to quickly grant interim security and enable the U.N and other humanitarian agencies access to Kachin refugees in Yunnan province.

Though Myanmar is on the path of economic liberalization and expansion, the Kachin area has not profited due to the continuing struggle. Scarcity of economic possibilities for the Kachins forces them to traverse into China for survival. The Kachins do not have entree to border passes, which is mandatory to enter China legitimately. They traverse the frontier as illegal migrants who cannot demand rights or benefits in China that has led to strains within the locals and migrants over the division of resources and job possibilities in future. Many Kachin families have turned back to Myanmar from Yunnan due to the lack of sufficient humanitarian support and the demand from Chinese officials. Theft, violence against women, and case killings are amongst the charges leveled against the militia. Landmines, recruiting children to fight and the deaths of thousands of Kachins have relocated many of them to largely China being nearby to the frontier. Also, many Kachins have moved to encampments in close by Southeast Asian nations.

China has been using ethnic conflicts to gain over opposition state parties, where it has become more outspoken in Myanmar's peace process. A report indicating a Myanmar senior official connected in the peace process blamed China of attempting to thwart Myanmar's peace process. He blamed China of freezing the United Wa State Army (UWSA) and the Kachin Independence Organization (KIO) from engaging in the peace agreement unless Myanmar welcomes the Myanmar National Democratic Alliance Army (MNDAA) into the process. Yun Sun of the Henry L. Stimson Center, for one, argues that the level of Chinese arbitration in Myanmar "directly equates with the intensity of the conflict and its spillover impact." It shows qualm on China and its objective to primarily lessen cross-border impacts of the disputes and to assure border protection and security. China's fundamental aims towards Myanmar's ethnic frictions in the initial stage seems to have been restricted and originally concerned with boundary protection and security. It seemed convinced that the political revolutions inside Myanmar would not alter its strategic interests in the borderlands. China wields direct as well as indirect influence with several stakeholders in Myanmar. The foreign policy of China towards Myanmar is increasingly regulated toward stoking economic and industrial expansion at home, especially through the procurement of energy and natural reserves to boost the economy of Yunnan. Amidst the resumption of hostilities between the Kachins and the Burmese army in 2011, there has been a constant inrush of refugees into China. The displaced Kachins are compelled to take sanctuary in China due to a lack of humanitarian assistance and security in their land. China had initially engaged in the discussions within the Burma government and the KIO in Myitkyina.

The Kachin area adjoins China's Yunnan Province and is its biggest trading partner. Non-refoulement is the foundation of refugee security.

It is foundational to China's statutory responsibilities toward refugees. The principal protection granted to refugees is against refoulement. The Refugee Convention prevents the forced return in any of the circumstances of refugees to countries or places where their life or right would be endangered concerning their race, religion, nationality, and the society of an appropriate social or political opinion. The Refugee Convention obligates states to grant to refugees the same treatment as is granted to citizens regarding fundamental education. At present, the bulk of activity between Kachin and Yunnan is made up of unauthorized migration of refugees and illegal trading. Also, several children had no admittance to schools and the establishments lacked the necessary amenities and health care. The Kachins are also facing hurdles of paying rent in Yunnan and in some neighborhoods, the Kachins are seen utilizing deserted or abandoned area without having to pay rent. Chinese central government and Yunnan provincial authorities have usually permitted Kachins to enter and reside in China. Still, some Kachins have been denied entry at the outposts and local authorities under the regulation of central officials have pushed others back. There are an approximated several thousand Kachins residing Yunnan, as per local aid channels. However, the number of refugees is unknown who are not residing in the camps or shared surroundings, whose information has not been gathered. Kachins in Yunnan have recounted to HRW the daunting, perils, and exploitations they have suffered from the Burmese army. Kachins are exposed to ill treatment by local employers and have been subjected to unreasonable drug experimentation and continued detainment by the Chinese officials.

As per the HRW, the Kachin refugees in Yunnan promulgated that they had obtained no humanitarian support from the Chinese government and several humanitarian firms have had no entree to the refugees following 2011. The Chinese government has also not permitted UNHCR and other foreign humanitarian organizations access since the time they initially came. UNHCR aboveboard concedes that it encounters barriers in applying its mandate in China and ascribes this to the government's difference of refugee matters usually. Many Kachin refugees in Yunnan interviewed by HRW displayed a longing to return to Myanmar, but at the cost of their lives. In contemporary times, fighting has swelled up repeatedly despite recurring cease-fires and iterated rounds of mediation. Till today, private Kachin aid channels working in Yunnan have held the role in rendering humanitarian aid for the refugees. The Kachin-led establishment "Wunpawng Ninghtoi", an ad-hoc channel created when the struggle started, has been a prominent humanitarian player for the Kachins in Yunnan. Human rights activists have documented grounds of horrendous exploitations of Kachins by the Burmese followed later by the Myanmar militia.

Following the 2011 Kachin brawl of reiterated repugnance within the Myanmar militia and the KIA, some of the displaced Kachins were denied access into China or vigorously sent back to Myanmar that put them in great jeopardy and generated a pervading abhorrence of forced return amongst the Kachin refugees who live in Yunnan. HRW uses the phrase "refugee" for Kachin who have entered China post-2011 due to the armed dispute and rights violations in Kachin, who would endure grave perils to their lives if sent back to Kachin State. Since 2011, the well-armed dispute within the KIA and the Myanmar government has expanded to neighboring northerly Shan State, where the Chinese and Myanmar governments likewise have vital economic gains such as transnational gas and oil pipelines connecting China and westward Myanmar. This 500-mile extended twofold pipelines will support China to increase its economy in the landlocked Yunnan while making billions in profits for the Myanmar government. The pipeline will also facilitate the Chinese state to import oil from Africa and the Middle East, avoiding the Straits of Malacca, a crucial oil transportation path that is exposed to security perils. The Kachin who fled to Yunnan since 2011 covers several children in want of education. The Convention on the Rights of the Child, to which China is party, assures that basic education is "free and compulsory for all," that also includes the refugee children who are considered undocumented refugees support their right to education. A spokesperson from the Chinese government in 2012, pointed to the Kachin refugees in Yunnan as "border residents" rather than refugees, maintaining that most come to visit friends and kin.

Kachin refugees, who reside in Yunnan, have faced several health problems, as they are helpless to afford health care and medication in

Yunnan. Though local officials have interviewed the refugees about their intentions for fleeing Burma and collected their necessary biographical data, the Chinese government has not met its responsibilities to give government aid or to permit UNHCR and other humanitarian organizations to help the refugees and grant them food and other essential items. The dispute has also led to human trafficking near the Sino-Myanmar border. Young women and girls uprooted by the conflict are traded to Chinese men or families as brides and bonded workers, as per the report by the Kachin Women's Association Thailand (KWAT). Despite the Myanmar officials setting up anti-trafficking units, the condition has not improved. A joint mechanism to fight human trafficking in the boundary zones has yet to be developed by both nations. China has become the Kachin area's single casement to the external world. Several of the refugees have been in China for a longer time and unfortunately, their supplies are falling out. The open-ended Kachin dispute in Burma acts as a hurdle for China in controlling its frontier regions, though the Chinese government has allowed most Kachin refugees to enter and reside in Yunnan and has also enabled some small local nongovernmental institutions to assist. The disinclination of China to accommodate these refugees official status causes many to assume they do not have a right to the refuge that makes them more susceptive to forceful return. Additionally, Immigrant workers in China are expected to hold work visas or foreign resident documents. China's law restricts the rights to own legally obtained income, savings, homes and other legal property to Chinese nationals.

China should spring up and acknowledge that it has responsibilities, after ratifying the refugee convention and its protocol. It should carry out regular transparent assessments concerning the living situation, provide essential needs, investigate violations and abuses, basic education and protect the Kachins against refoulement and permit them to remain in China by providing work. China should likewise give untrammelled admittance to refugees by regional and worldwide organizations such as the UNHCR, to grant safeguard and humanitarian support.

CHAPTER 10

The Forgotten Kokangs

A few years ago, the unforeseen fury of hostilities in northerly Shan State's isolated Kokang region had caught the world's attention. Majority of the Kokangs are descendants of China who moved to the Shan State of Myanmar in the 18th century. The Yang clan, a Chinese army group that escaped with the Ming supporters from Nanjing to Yunnan Province, and later relocated to the Shan State created a feudal state called Kokang in the mid-17th century. The huge bulk of citizens are ethnic Chinese, using the Yuan currency and speaking the Chinese language. The area was extremely poor economically and the paucity of water and huge mountains made rice farming practically unthinkable, so the citizens had to hinge on to two yields, opium and tea. Under the 1897 Beijing Convention, the Kokang area conceded to the British, which may appear odd given its ethnic synthesis. Myanmar's administration was even little successful compared to the British in bringing the Kokangs under centralized check. During this time Yunnan was not completely dominated by the ruler in China, and due to Kokang's vicinity to Hsenwi in Shan State, trade and commerce oftentimes progressed west side rather than the eastern side. Virtually, the whole Konkang region was taken control by Kuomintang (KMT) forces at the beginning of 1950s, while the Chinese communists drove the nationalists to escape athwart the frontier. The Kokang unit came to be known as the MNDAA. The Kokang struggle provoked a public condemnation from China, where the Burmese regime, wrecked the rights and interests of Chinese civilians living there.

Between the 1960s and 1989, the region was governed by the CPB. The communist control in 1968 changed Kokang culturally and politically. The former rulers escaped and the land they left back was allocated to landless farmers. Law and order were reconstructed after ages of chaos and anarchy. However, there was one significant quandary where CPB could not resolve, the cultivation of Opium. The regional farmers, at the base of the socio-economic step-stool, could not make their mints from a crop like opium due to CPB's complexity of discovering suitable crops for the region who later became less interested in deciding an adequate replacement due to cut of Chinese assistance in following 1970s. The CPB mutiny led to ethnic tensions in 1989 and soon expanded to other CPB areas. The 1989 revolt marked yet another economic and social change of the areas, near the frontier of China. Following its end in 1989, Kokang became a distinctive region of Myanmar.

Like the Kachins, Kokangs in China have to face the risk of persecution and ill treatment upon return to Myanmar, as the 1951 Convention description of a refugee makes no distinction between refugees escaping peacetime or wartime persecution. Though China's acceptance of Kachins and Kokangs is in front with UNHCR guidelines for dealing with large-scale inrushes of uprooted people, the UNHCR office in China that usually administers the RSD, have not been permitted to move to the boundary zones where the Kachins and Kokangs live. It has likewise not been possible for displaced Kachins and Kokangs in Yunnan to register with UNHCR or apply for refugee status via the UNHCR conducted RSD procedure.

In 2009, roughly 37,000 commoners entered Yunnan from Laukkai, the capital of Kokang in Shan State, Myanmar, due to the armed conflict and disagreements within the Myanmar government troops and the MNDAA. However, the displaced Kokangs were later willingly repatriated and the encampments were pulled out. Following 2009, more than 100,000 ethnic Kachins and Kokangs have traversed into Yunnan, to escape armed dispute in Kachin and Shan State. The Chinese officials consequently established camps and thousands of temporary shelters and provided essential needs to host the relocated Kokangs in various provinces of Yunnan. But the refugees who were not accepted in the camps did not usually receive support from the Chinese government and had to depend on the assistance from NGOs, individual contributions and their resources. Further, in 2015 when an armed conflict recommenced within the MNDAA and the Myanmar government troops, many thousands of civilians yet again escaped to Yunnan from Laukkai. As of 2017, several of the uprooted Kokangs endured in Yunnan with minimal support from Chinese officials and the global community. Kokangs are also subject to human right abuses that include deadly firings, home intrusions, violence, torment and forced labor.

China wants the Kokang to be included in the comprehensive peace negotiations that Aung San Suu Kyi initiated. However, in 2016, U

Thein Swe, the Union Minister for Labor, Immigration and Population announced that he declined to relax the terms of the controversial 1982 Citizenship Law concerning the Kokang inhabitants. Thein further stated that the jeopardy of fraudulent impersonation or concealment by those appealing for citizenship was too prominent. The civil disorder or instability is a setback to attempts by Aung San Suu Kyi, Myanmar's de facto leader to attain a general peace settlement with Myanmar's ethnic minorities where some of them show rebellions and resistance bridging over decades. Though the Chinese officials declared that they rendered required support in compliance with community practices based on humanitarianism, there is no indication that they did so enough. It is crucial to apprehend that in the Kokang armed friction in 2009, 2015 and till date, the Chinese officials attributed to the relocated Kokangs in Yunnan as 'border residents' and refused to accept the fact that they were refugees.

The 1997 agreement on Chinese–Myanmar Border Management and partnership within China and Myanmar describes 'border residents' as 'persons with habitual residence in border areas of each party'. The 1997 Chinese–Myanmar Agreement permits border dwellers to traverse the border with an exit-entry pass exempting them from standard visa necessities. The exit-entry permit authorizes the possessor to traverse the frontier and move within the border regions specified in the agreement. The 1990 Yunnan Rules also permits the border citizens from Myanmar to enter China without a valid passport and exempt them from getting an ordinary Chinese visa which is usually needed for Myanmar inhabitants. Nevertheless, when the 1997 Chinese–Myanmar agreement shows a hollow, for instance, such as the stay of the border residents in Yunnan, the 1990 Yunnan Rules apply. While many of the Kachins and Kokangs did possess an exit-entry permit announced by Myanmar immigration officials when they left to Yunnan, several others did not. The exit-entry permits provided by the Myanmar immigration officials in Kachin State, considered to be a 'highly political and policy-oriented' issue do not particularize the objectives such as time period of the permit, paid employment during the interim stay, procedure to obtain the permit for which the possessor traverses or is authorized to pass the boundary. Both Kachins and Kokangs are unable to avail the rights to interim stay in China under article 46 of the 2012 Exit and Entry Administration Law. Hence, where there is a dispute betwixt the 1997 Chinese–Myanmar deal and the 1990 Yunnan Rules, the 1997 Chinese–Myanmar deal should preponderate.

China's unwillingness to permit UNHCR to access the relocated refugees is also discrepant with its consignment under article 35 of the Refugee Convention, as well as article 3(5) of the 1995 China–UNHCR Agreement, to collaborate with UNHCR in the performance of its objectives.

While China does not have a national RSD tool, the lack of domestic RSD process is no justification for its negligence to permit evaluation of the specific details of the uprooted Kokangs and Kachins. China's refutation of refugee status to the displaced Kokangs and Kachins without proper assessment led to the forced repatriation of many refugees. The ambivalence has also disengaged relations between China and Myanmar, where the former views as a pivotal passageway in its "Belt and Road Initiative" (BRI) maneuvering to boost economic interconnections connecting China and other countries which are part of BRI. China should be a peacemaker and observer to support in the dispute resolution. China should review its refugee policies thoroughly in a constructive manner towards Myanmar as the Suu Kyi government takes over yet again in the 2020 election.

The Rohingya Fiasco

The memoirs of various countries are formed by horrific stories that cover well-organized mass killings, cruelty and brutal repression. The barbarity of such circumstances is challenging to understand. But explaining why such incidents take place, what influence they have on the nation and communities, and how they may be checked in future is very essential. Nearly a million Rohingya Muslims have escaped their homeland due to aggressive operations and genocide conducted by the security forces of Myanmar that include massacre, abduction, violence against women and children and incendiarism. The concept of "Genocide" became a part of the International criminal law in 1951 when the United Nations Convention on the Prevention and Punishment of the Crime of Genocide (UNGC) came into force. Hence, Article 1 of the UNGC states that nations adhering to the UNGC recognize genocide as a crime under international law, which they try to stop and to punish. Burma attacks on Arakan were numerous and cruel, damaging mosques, archives, libraries and cultural establishments. The Rohingyas reside in Rakhine (Arakan) state, sharing a frontier with Bangladesh and divided from Burma by the Arakan Yoma mountain ranges. They are the descendants of diverse foreign traders and soldiers most prominently Turkish, Arab, Mongol, Bengali and Portuguese, who started settling down in Arakan after the ninth century, merging with several indigenous tribes. It was in the 15th century when the Rohingyas converted to Islam when Arakan was a feudatory of Bengal. During this time they acquired their distinguished art and culture following which Arakan was suppressed at several occasions where the armies of Burma and Portugal left the region impoverished and depopulated.

After the conquering by the British East India Company, Arakan became one of the parts of British India and drew settlers from the neighboring Chittagong Division of the Bengal Presidency. It became a division of British Burma in 1937. Throughout World War II the Rohingyas continued to remain loyal to the British, even when they retreated into India. However, the will-o'-the-wisp of Rohingya autonomy and sovereignty was short-lived. Due to this choice of being loyal to the British, the Rohingya ended up paying a high price for this decision when the imperial Japanese forces and Burma troops abused, tortured and massacred thousands of Rohingyas and nearly 22,000 refugees escaped to India. The Rakhine (Arakan) state was later fused into the newly independent state of Burma when the 1948 treaty granted Burma liberation from Britain. Thereafter Burma-Rohingya ties that were not very friendly or pleasant began to worsen rapidly. Rohingya refugees who had lived in India following the war were not allowed to return to Burma.

In 1962 when Ne Win became Burma's head of the state, he put forth the "Operation dragon king" in 1978, against nonnatives or foreigners in Burma who were targeted including the Rohingya. Following 1982, the citizenship law was announced which didn't approve Rohingya to be part of citizenship. In 1988, Aung San Suu Kyi led a democracy crusade against military rule. Ne win stepped down but State Law and order Restoration Council (SLORC) crumpled the insurgency and restored military rule by killing thousands. SLORC in the year 1990, conducted elections in Rakhine assuming the Rohingya will support the government. But they didn't and there were sit-ins and protests everywhere in Burma. In 1991, SLORC began "Operation clean" and "Beautiful nation". In the year 1992, Burma formed "NaSaKa", an immigration police force that was engaged in unmerciful and continuing human rights violations against the Rohingya.

What the U.N has considered being an act in "Ethnic Cleansing" has resulted in the Rohingya refugees being forced into temporary camps in bordering Bangladesh. Being one of the most impoverished and most thickly populated nations in Asia, Bangladesh cannot afford to provide shelter to a million Rohingyas. Despite the assistance rendered by foreign agencies, the Rohingyas are left in dreadful situations, the victims of food shortages, disease and flood rains. The voluntary and involuntary action repatriation of the Rohingya began after Myanmar and Bangladesh signed a repatriation treaty in 1992. The Myanmar and Bangladeshi governments, in the beginning of 1992, with the engagement of the UNHCR allowed a proposal to permit the return of some Muslims to Arakan. Implementation of the agreement nevertheless quickly faced obstacles. In 1993, Burmese authorities subsequently accepted to provide the UNHCR access to Rohingyas who were repatriated from Bangladesh and to permit global monitoring of the human rights condition in Arakan. The SLORC also declined to enable monitoring by the UNHCR of refugees' protection once the refugees were back in Burma. The UNHCR quickly retracted its assistance for the agreement and the global community-directed that repatriations would not begin till the U.N observers could ensure the refugees' "safe and voluntary" return. Rohingya inside the camps acknowledged immediately by demurring the repatriation plan however the protests stopped when Bangladeshi troops shot a crowd of around 2,000 refugees, killing one and wounding twenty. The Bangladeshi and Myanmar authorities immediately rejected the proposed repatriations momentarily. The refugees were exposed to people smugglers and human traffickers. Where there are no refugee encampments, they experience inadequate assistance and are routinely subjected to detention, prejudice, harassment and exploitative working situations. The most current mass outflow of refugees happened when more than 14,500 Rohingya have escaped to Bangladesh between January and November 2018 to flee the continuing oppression and brutality in Myanmar, combining almost 1 million others from 2017 and previous years in dangerous, congested camps. Situation continues to remain dreadful for the numbered 500,000-600,000 Rohingyas who still reside in Rakhine.

China shares a border with Myanmar besides being an important trading ally. However, it hasn't urged Myanmar on its handling of the Rohingya or performed a crucial function in attempts to resettle them. Even though in 2016 China attempted to help tackle a diplomatic dispute between Bangladesh and Myanmar over the situation of Rohingya, China that could perform a leading role however was not fit to take an opinion on this issue, as China believes this would harm the bilateral engagements among the countries. China has abstained from reprimanding Myanmar being next-door-neighbor putting the national interest into play. China needs to be more vigilant in preserving its strategic and economic leverage over its neighbors rather than reprimand them over human rights concerns.

China as a rising global power should nurture regional collaboration being a significant international investor in Myanmar. It had pressed Myanmar to take measures in the repatriation of the Rohingya refugees asserting that it attributes vast attention to the Rohingya plight. China has previously been an arbitrator in Rohingya problem but it hasn't come to the world stage to address a long-lasting resolution for the issue. According to Forbes, China is principally against the notion of universal human rights and rather has strategic and trade interests in Myanmar. China's relative quietude on the Rohingya issue likely yields from its trade benefits in the Rakhine. Yun Sun, a Chinese scholar from Brookings Institution, Washington, mentioned that the Rohingya and other refugee communities which are not of Chinese ethnicity are less of an interest to Beijing. China despite being the second largest economy is still a developing nation with a low income that is grappling with 16.6 million poor people who are expecting monetary aid.

Though China has the economic capacity to mediate the Rohingya issue, it regards the Rohingya plight as an economic predicament, given that its solution is concentrated on advancement. China must continue to urge international organizations and also encourage nations with a greater financial capacity to assist the Rohingyas to find an alternative solution for their resettlement. Any plan can hardly make inadequate progress unless Myanmar is compliant to roll back the institutional checks that render Rohingya as secondary-class communities. While economic support is crucial, the actual quandary is arguably deeply political, and there needs to be an accompanying political resolution. Unless the Rohingyas are received as equal citizens of Myanmar, it is unlikely that there will be a long-lasting solution to the Rakhine crisis.

CHAPTER 12

Hong Kong in a Cleft Stick

China has in many ways molded Hong Kong in the past decades but it has had limited influence on the handling of refugees in Hong Kong. Historically, the region has been a mixed platter in protecting refugees. The refugees have made important waves entering Hong Kong due to conflicts and wars and the region's traditional role as a trading and transit entrepôt. Hong Kong became a colony of the British Empire after the Qing dynasty ceded it at the end of the First Opium War in 1842. Later, the whole region was transferred over to China in 1997 under the system of "one country, two systems".

Hong Kong has not been part of the 1951 Convention and hence, refugees are helpless to take advantage of the different of socio-economic benefits. Regardless of not being associated with the convention, following the 1950s, the state has allowed refuge seekers access in the times. The U.K mentioned the region's "sui generis" features in discountenancing to extend the Refugee Convention such as economic successfulness, tiny size and closeness to developing or less developed nations. The following features especially made Hong Kong exposed to economic migration and unlawful entry of asylum seekers. The "one country two systems" formula meant that Hong Kong manages its policy towards refugees in the region. But Hong Kong is a party to the International Covenant on Civil and Political Rights (ICCPR) and International Covenant on Economic, Social and Cultural Rights (ICESCR). ICESCR aims at providing basic socio-economic rights like an essential quality of life in a spectrum of areas including water, food, health care education and shelter. The ICCPR is pertinent in evaluating the validity of the government's refugee social welfare and work support systems. Both the ICCPR and ICESCR on whole give a source of rights that refugees can depend on in claiming socio-economic prerogatives to an extent. However, social welfare prerequisites provided to refugees is inadequate, considering that Hong Kong has one of the most upscale rental markets globally. There are also several NGOs in Hong Kong who additionally grant assistance in a spectrum of areas consisting of education and healthcare, the provision of accommodations, rent and living allowances.

In 1949, the Chinese Civil War led to the region's population expanding from 600,000 to 2.1 million. Between the 1940s and 1980s, Occidental nations actively supported flows of refugees, particularly from communist nations. Hong Kong, with a liberal visa regime to boost tourism, admitted a more substantial proportion of refugees its community when compared to China or Japan, however, the number is quite minute. Through the 'Touch Base' policy in the late 1970s, the ethnic Chinese from Mainland China who landed in Hong Kong without being detained were granted Hong Kong identity cards. The ethnic Chinese today make up the largest population in Hong Kong and have resided here due to numerous economic opportunities. Russians in Hong Kong were considered as region's more diminutive groups of refugees and an insignificant part of the global Russian diaspora where many Russians from China between the 1950s and 1970s crossed through Hong Kong on their way to resettlement in Australia, Canada and other countries. After PRC was established, the Russians dwelling in Shanghai, China began to depart.

Several Vietnamese people in the mid-1970s, in Hong Kong relocated as an outcome of the Vietnam War and mistreatment. Hong Kong in 1979 adopted the "port of first asylum policy" and welcomed over 100,000 Vietnamese at the zenith of migration in the late 1980s and several refugee camps were set up. Due to the humanitarian policy of the Hong Kong Government and under the responsibility of the U.N, some Vietnamese were allowed to dwell in Hong Kong. The unlawful entry of Vietnamese refugees was a predicament, which later gave Hong Kong a hard time for multiple years. Nevertheless, the difficulty was settled in the year 2000. Following 2004, after a string of decisions by Hong Kong courts prevented the immigration authority from the departure of any unauthorized immigrants as long as those people alleged mistreatment or danger of torment and expected arbitration of their rights. Since 2004, there was a striking rise of applicants in the number of refuge seekers and torture. In 2014–15, the amount of refuge seeker applicants towered, multiplying by 70% under the Unified Screening Mechanism (USM) administrated by the Department of Immigration. Due to this mechanism, UNHCR had halted the screening of refuge applications under its charge in Hong Kong and the following two processes were not to be managed independently by the UNHCR regarding refuge seekers who alleged danger of persecution and government of Hong Kong evaluating allegations of inhumanity perils. Hong Kong's policy to hand over the probe of refugee applications to the UNHCR was the case of a legal hurdle in Prabakar v Secretary for Security, where the government had to begin its evaluation and adopt high standards of procedural justice where in a person cases that their repatriation would place them in jeopardy of being abused. Therefore, in the Prabakar case, the government formulated its own mechanism to screen torture claims and the refugees arriving in Hong Kong had two promenades to affirm protection from refoulement, which is either under Hong Kong's Torture Convention or the Refugee Convention of UNHCR.

The refugees' form a disadvantaged group where unlike the nationals they do not have the same chance to gain a satisfactory standard of living based on their efforts. The living standards of Hong Kong are considered more high-priced than economically flourishing Asian nations like Korea and occidental nations where refugee social welfare terms are considerably more acceptable. Hong Kong has been a crucial juncture in the area of refugee protection. Turbulence has been a cause of refugee swells in the region, who have been long attracted in search of a better life and escaping persecution. The refugees are not permitted to work and are also being refused the opening to blend into the society and forge bonds with the external world. There are systemic stoppages in RSD and complexities in being resettled. Several refugees have no other alternative except to reside in Hong Kong for extended periods expecting a long-lasting resolution. The refugee children in Hong Kong are not qualified to study in the public schools given their unlawful status and the Government does not acknowledge the right to education. Hence, there is an absence of a definite policy to allow school admissions to these children. Likewise, adults cannot obtain educational assistance dismissing them of opportunities for self-development and social incorporation through their long stay. There are also significant concerns especially for the mental health of refugees.

The Hong Kong government continues to state that it has no statutory responsibility to support refugees rather affirming that any welfare assistance the government does give is conferred on a discretional humanitarian basis. The application processing of asylum seekers takes ten or more years for their requests to be processed, a wait that is time testing as compared to other nations which take considerably less processing time. Approximately only 5-10% of asylum seekers achieved refugee status from the UNHCR in Hong Kong. In case UNHCR sends them to a different country, if one is allowed as a refugee, this is a move towards finally becoming a subject of the nation one has been resettled in. Several asylum seekers in Hong Kong also believe that the only way they can take the edge off from being a refugee is to get married to a local. Nevertheless, since asylum seekers have no proper jobs and no accepted place in society, this sounds easier than done. Asylum seekers tend to reside in low-cost accommodations due to the basic level of rental support given by the Hong Kong government and the remarkably high price of rent in the city but asylum seekers in the countryside have found more affordable accommodation. Bureaucratic frailty is also one cause for the interminable setbacks in the processing of asylum-seeker matters.

Successful applicants show that the refugees are not provided with any kind of lawful residence and can simply appeal for a permit for a six-month duration for employment. In 2012, Hong Kong Immigration Department spokesperson stated that the region has a long-established policy of not allowing refugees and do not accept people looking for refugee status indicating alarms that refugees would harm the system given the affluence of the region's liberal visa system and economic growth. The South China Morning Post stated that some refugees are driven to make claims to unlawfully working in Hong Kong for years. Refugees have also been linked with a soaring level of street crime. For instance, in 2015, a string of arrests of many suspects broke a major drug syndicate functioning in Hong Kong mostly labeled as refugees from Gambia, Africa. Vision First, a refugee advocacy NGO, bickers that criminal movement by refugees is due to Hong Kong's bungled refuge policy that gives meager welfare support and restricts working. There is also visible racism in Hong Kong with white people oftentimes treated more favorably than other races in daily intercommunications. Unfortunately, Hong Kong racism is usually censured in mass media. As per the 2013 World Values Survey, 27% of Hongkongers would not want to have a neighbor of a diverse race, pointing to wonder among analysts. But the lack of racism amongst young Hongkongers specified by asylum seekers, have been effective during the Umbrella Movement who have been sympathetic.

In 2017, there were approximately 14,000 refugee seekers awaiting resolution of their applications with over half of them from South Asian nations, 10% from Africa and nearly a third from South East Asia. The UNHCR has been an influential provider of assistance to mandated refugees in the form of living allowances but there has been a variation in the level of support in recent years where the UNHCR chose to reallocate its support to approach continuing refugee crises in more unsafe and exposed regions across the globe. Necessary steps have been taken to bring Hong Kong's refugee screening methods into the front with global statutory standards since last one decade. Legally imposed 'high measure of fairness' has directed to fundamental system amelioration for the refugees to evade persecution or ominous human rights violations.

Hong Kong has changed following China's imposition of the new security law in 2020. The city, which for decades had been a region of refuge for people fleeing conflict, political persecution, human right abuses, famine in mainland China is presently a semi-autonomous city and has made many Hongkongers fleeing other nations. Earlier, Article 23 of Hong Kong's Basic Law presented that Hong Kong Special Administrative Region (HKSAR) established rules on its own for the region's security and prevented political groups outside HKSAR from interfering in the region's independent security. Today, constitutional rights and habeas corpus have been at the core of Hong Kong's continuing crackdown against Chinese efforts to declare pressing control over the territory. The New national security law will largely threaten the rule of law in Hong Kong, limiting the right to due process, curbing freedom of speech and diminishing other fundamental civil liberties. Many pro-democracy activists have been detained and some have fled to other nations including Taiwan that is close by and ethnically Chinese with democratic self-rule. Though Taiwan does not have a refugee law, it has in the past handled Mainland Chinese asylum seekers on a case-by-case footing and prudently. President Tsai Ing-wen's administration also started a new government office to assist business investors and Hong Kong activists to emigrate. Amnesty International in Mainland China has documented the government's customary practice of subversion onsets to detain reporters, advocates, academicians and activists. In Western governments, they have been welcomed as refugees fleeing China's squeezing grip over Hong Kong. The young activists, part of the Umbrella Movement, many who have never even travelled to China, showed Sinophobic scornfulness and resentment towards the Chinese Mainland stating that Hong Kong was better under the British. Some of Hong Kong activists have been given asylum in the U.S, Canada and Germany lately due to western nations' stand on the infringement of human rights that has become a ground for degenerating associations between China and the West. The Hong Kong Public Opinion Programme 2017 report found that Hongkongers recognize themselves more as Hongkongers, Asians, and global citizens than as subjects of PRC. Boris Johnson, the Prime Minister of the U.K who criticized the new security law, that has disrupted Hong Kong's freedom has proposed the opportunity for the Hong Kongers to settle in the U.K and eventually apply for citizenship. The Government of U.K is also preparing for a 100 per cent rise in the amount of Hong Kong nationals arriving in Britain after Johnson offered nearly three million people shelter.

Lately, the refugees in Hong Kong have dwindled from 10,922 in 2015 to 8,956 in 2017 due to an increasing amount of deportations with no optimism in attaining refugee status, with an approval rate of scarcer than 1%. The new law security will have major consequences that can likewise see a further dip in the number of asylum seekers in Hong Kong in the coming years. The asylum seekers residing presently can have a tough time in adjusting with the law. Through the new law, people could be taken to Mainland China for unfair trials impacting human rights protection, as the investigating officials will have new and broad powers. Carrie Lam, the Hong Kong Chief Executive has frequently forced towards restricting human rights in the name of national security that would infringe global standards.

The asylum seekers had been symbols for some Hong Kong young activists of the region's continuing anti Chinese stand. Some asylum seekers have taken on a socially and symbolically vital task for some of the region's youngsters. As the CPC tries to enforce strict control on the security law, the asylum seekers would likely be further cornered with more socio-economic restrictions imposed on them. After inviting chagrin from the rest of the world due to the COVID pandemic negligence, China must consider a consensus decision-building process in order to maintain peace, stability and uphold human rights in the region. The Chinese government must bring in new schemes for the betterment of the existing refugees by providing them with an opportunity to improve education and job skills, form human links and to attain social synthesis. There is a need to take steps to assure that refugees are socially blended into the Hong Kong society irrespective of ethnicity.

CHAPTER 13

The COVID Pandemic Dust
An Epilogue

China as a mounting power is examining the existing global order with its fast-growing economic strength, extensive global investment, burgeoning military capability and superior technology apart from aggressively expanding its foreign influence at the world platform. Today, the Chinese adventurism and expansionism on sea and land have been oxygenating China. It is now poised to deploy its military and economic strengths to advance its national interest on numerous fronts in a naked and unhindered way. China wants a global order with Chinese characters where liberal values are of little value as a course of action for human advancement and development. The Chinese recalcitrance and its complete readiness to progress its interests is contrary to the grain of international law, diplomatic negotiations and codes of conduct- China believes that their sun has risen and will not set now.

State power is now determined not only in military terms but also in economic terms. China's ascension signals for the first time in over hundreds of years that an alternative non-Western power, a preceding sufferer of Western or Japanese colonialism, is attempting its position in the ranks of great global leadership. Nevertheless, accelerated economic growth of nations like China also indicated that actors arose in the international sphere due to their expanding economic clout that presently have a voice in international relations. Before taking over as 'numero uno', China wants to challenge the status quo and national interests. Its 'core interest diplomacy' is the fundamental step to expose its nuts and bolts position for a future partnership that should be engaged with great caution. Following the 2008 global recession, China pulled off its hood of 'peaceful rise', by showing its true appearance of expansionism and hostility. China's economic bouncebackability became apparent after it drove over the 2008 global crisis moderately safe, and through the years it grew more prepared to advance itself, notably following President Xi Jinping. During the 19th National Congress of the CPC in 2017, Xi Jinping announced that, while Mao Zedong affirmed China's liberation from colonialism and Deng actualized economic prosperity and reforms, Xi would make China powerful again in the 21st century. Xi's rise to leadership was a turning period in China's foreign policy rulings.

The persona of China as an authoritarian government headed by a closed-door CPC presents a truculent and belligerent force for the world. China's disinclination to play by international rules makes its 'not so peaceful' rise a focus of deep interest. The Chinese dragon consumes a lot of time agonizing on what other nations hold of it. Several international relations theories had foretold various outcomes of China's future and still continue to do so. The evolution of a new post of leadership (in the case of China) has appeared often in severe alterations in the foreign political fabrications that have eventually resulted in war, is well manifested within the offensive realism of international relations that is the 'Theory of hegemonic stability'. The rise of China as an important actor in global politics has begun to question the old hegemony of the U.S.

China asserts that its decisions on foreign policy questions infer from its "Five Principles of Peaceful Coexistence" such as mutual non-aggression, non-interference in each other's internal affairs, mutual benefit, and peaceful coexistence, mutual respect for sovereignty and territorial integrity, equality. China's "peaceful rise" strategy was originally proposed to counter perceptions of a "China peril". The idea of "peaceful rise" was an ordered policy, which arose under the administration of Hu Jintao. The term was an effort to refute abreast of the "China threat theory". The "peaceful rise" approach endeavored to portray China as a reliable global player, highlighting its soft power and that China is necessitated to its domestic matters by enhancing the well-being requirements of its citizens before intervening in foreign affairs.

While China continues to sneeze post-COVID-19, it seems to be giving migraine to the whole world. The post-COVID world has also already held China culpable for all the miseries that both the Chinese citizens and the global population have encountered. It has intensified its aggressiveness against India, U.S, and so on ever since the virus outbreak. The 'geopolitical migraine' that has gotten on the nerves of the contemporary world due to China is an indication that the 'Thucydides trap', exists which indicates that China's rise is unquestionably 'not peaceful'. China describes itself as a "Third World" nation that seeks an "independent" foreign policy of peace.

"Independence" here indicates that China does not align itself with any other major power.

By the Third World, it means that China is a developing nation and not part of any power bloc such as that around the U.S or the socialist bloc previously associated with the Soviet Union. China which is on the brink on working in achieving 'superpower status' by giving into sharp power, land grabs, it is proceeding into disputed waters, asserting its maritime claims, changing the rules of the international order, the trade war with the U.S, Taiwan's independence aspirations being thwarted and the new imposition of the Hong Kong law, the Huawei issue, debt traps, COVID-19 cover-up, declining soft power propaganda, economic exploitation etc., has inflated concerns which indicate 'not a peaceful rise' for the Chinese dragon to navigate and its fire of fury might be extinguished by the rest of the world.

Under Deng Xiaoping, Chinese foreign policy was directed by the adage 'hide your strength and bide your time', however under Xi, China is no longer hiding anything, nor is it biding its time. It wants to achieve its place in the sun, and it wants to do so soon. China's repressive politics has proved disastrous for the country including the refugees. The Chinese Professor Xu Zhangrun of Tsinghua University in this setting stated that "China has reached a 'dead-end' and democracy is the only way out." It is of no astonishment that Prof Xu is presently under house confinement with his Internet network disconnected.

Like how Nye states that power is the "means of obtaining desired outcomes" China has used its foreign policy of non-interference to augment influence in various countries. However, in 2017, the National Endowment for Democracy proposed the concept of 'Sharp Power'. It refers to a regime's capacity to influence the thoughts and opinions of audiences in a target nation to change their behavior and minds to undermine the political system of a target country using manipulative diplomatic policies. China beyond the borders has exhibited the kind of government by pursuing a grand craft using sharp power to promote its global interests by manipulating the political landscape of nations. China's efforts in transnational economic aid, cultural activities, people-to-people exchange, educational program and the advancement of foreign media operations are all run as a toolbox of sharp power.

China should consider following, Winston Churchill's "Jaw-jaw is better than war-war" way in dealing with other nations. It must ensure that its rise should be conducted in a way that does not disturb the relative harmony and security of the world. China should consider conducting "Careful Diplomacy" with nation-states or it might end up facing further backlash from the world and the realization of the great rejuvenation of the 'Chinese dream' and the goal to turn China into a leading global power in the future will remain a dream. China's rise cannot be peaceful unless the world leaders will promote China's further inclusion in the global system and regards China as part of the solution than an obstacle. Many experts have demonstrated that China uses "Nationalism" as a tool of foreign policy. Nationalism enables China to use conventional nationalist predilections to dodge showdown against perceived provocations when it anticipates that it is not in China's national interests.

Contemplating that Xi Jinping propelled a very grand strategy for the country as soon as he took over as China's president in 2013, one should anticipate anything less formidable soon. China has also advocated the elimination of the two-term limit on the presidency position, certainly acknowledging Xi Jinping to continue in power for life. In the book, 'Harmony and War: Confucian Culture and Chinese Power Politics', the author Dr. Yuan kan Wang postulates that China will slowly shift to an aggressive ambitious artifice after gaining ample horsepower. Mearsheimer's book titled the 'Tragedy of Great Power Politics', asserted that the ascension of China in the 21st centenary would be laden with hurdles.

While the world witnessed an outcry over the treatment of child asylum seekers by the former US President, Donald Trump due to the immigration policy that was controversial, on the deeper side, China has stated that it is against the idea of the country taking in the refugees. As China's economic and military clout has been growing, China seeks power and respect. As mentioned earlier chapters, despite being party to the 1951 Refugee Convention and the 1967 Protocol, China has no domestic definition of refugee. China being one of the 5 permanent members of the UNSC does not explicitly reject the UNHCR's authority for fear of jeopardizing its UNSC veto. However, that is not to say that China fully accepts to its mandate. China is a world power and has been modernizing itself in the recent decades. Ranging from their economy, cost friendly living expenses and universities, which are among world rankings, make it a promising place for refugees to escape the turmoil. The last time the CPC took large amount refugees was in 1979 where many people from Laos, Cambodia, and Vietnam moved to Southwest China who were of the Chinese ethnic origin but when thousands of Rohingya escaped Myanmar ethnic riots and poverty in 2015, China didn't take a stand on the worst humanitarian crisis in its own neighborhood and the world. The UNHCR offices are located in Beijing and Hong Kong, but China refuses to cooperate with systemizing and processing refugees within the country. Even when the popular Chinese actress Yao Chen (UNHCR goodwill ambassador) pushed for China to admit refugees on "Weibo" in June 2017, she met with public criticism. Many of the refugees who have obtained visas have found themselves trapped within the borders of China because of the fact that in order to obtain an exit visa, one must have the support of housing registrations. Which requires the refugees to have valid documents. This has lead to refugees purchasing of false documents and can easily lead to being arrested. Both of these methods will cost a great deal of money too.

China by accepting the UNHCR terms, fears the economic cost of providing the refugee services that the UNHCR championed and granting complete access to the UNHCR may expose China's poor treatment of refugees. According to global times, a poll, started circulating on the World Refugee Day 2018 on the social media platform Weibo, which found that 97.7 of almost 9000 respondents said they are opposed to China accepting foreign refugees. As per a Weibo user "China did not implement the family planning policy for decades to make room for refugees," The Chinese scholars feel that Washington is liable for creating such refugee problems and emphasis should be given on resettlement rather than repatriation. China's negligence of today's refugees portrays its image as an unwilling member in order to support the global community.

China aspires to be an emerging power among the global powers and it should take efforts to meet the international expectations like the refugee crisis. With a prematurely aging population just like Japan, it is going through a demographic crisis. The U.N projects that there will be 366 million older Chinese adults by 2050, which is substantially larger than the current total U.S. population (331 million). Though poverty and ageing remains an issue in China, Immigration could help prevent long-term economic stagnation associated with a shortage of young workers and a growing number of retired dependents. It must also aggrandize assistance via NGOs to the vulnerable refugees present in China. The UNHCR must continue to press the Chinese government for access to all of its the refugee populations.

Confucianism in China highlights on concepts like humanity, non-violence, Kindness, compassion, diligence, respect and responsibility in relationships. Confucius believed that people make up an important part of society. His concern for the disadvantage was seen in his teachings. For him society was deemed to provide assistance to the orphans and other deprived classes. The CPC has come to acknowledge that Confucius might be useful for them again to project China's soft power. China through the principles of Confucianism should move forward together in supporting the refugees and the global community stand on refugees so as to improve its stature and must consider all the refugees equal irrespective of the ethnicity. China has increasingly started to alter its refugee policies and artifices in contemporary years. China's inclination to guide and explore Asian explications will guide its strategy to disputes in the region. It must begin a consensus-building process with its neighboring states where all actors can undertake to fix the predicaments and conflicts by non-violent means. The most remarkable illustration is China's eagerness to play a third-party position in the Rohingya crisis. On April 1, 2020, Jiang Duan, an official at the Chinese mission in Geneva, was elected to work on the Consultative Group of UN Human Rights Council elected to Human Rights Council. This shows that China has a greater role to play concerning human rights and refugees in the near future. China's soft power has deteriorated drastically due to its several acts and the country that has invited further criticism across the world lately for mishandling of the virus must prove itself to come back on the track. Confucian philosophy presents the framework for the idea of win-win partnership and mutual benefit. Confucianism is at the rootstock of the description of "Chinese foreign aid" displaying the moral and idealistic components of China's foreign policy thinking. The Confucian frame determines the way Chinese foreign aid is practiced. Hence, China should consider increasing its foreign aid to support the refugees in and outside China. CPC should also consider establishing a separate governmental department to look after the welfare of the refugees. While the post-COVID world will see a huge surge in refugee crisis, a comprehensive review of China's refugee policy would be a good beginning. The post-COVID world presents a time for opportunity as well as a change for global cooperation.

References

Max Walden (2018), "Online polls show 97pc of Chinese reject accepting refugees", Asian Correspondent.

"Isolated in Yunnan, Kachin refugees in China's Yunnan Province", Human Rights Watch.

Myanmar events of 2018, Human Rights Watch.

Philip Wen (2015), "Myanmar's Kokang refugees caught between army, aged warlord and a pipeline to China", The Sydney Morning Herald.

Dr Fengshi Wu (2018), "China and the global refugee crisis", Centre for Contemporary Chinese Studies.

Myanmar: Kokang army recruiting Chinese nationals as mercenaries in Yunnan: Sources, Radio Free Asia

Tae-jun Kang (2019), "Death of North Korean Defector Sparks Concerns About South Korean Policies", The Diplomat.

"Figures at glance",UNHCR.

"Refugee Law and Policy In Selected Countries", The Law Library of Congress, Global Legal Research Center.

The People's Republic of China fact sheet of December 2015, UNHCR.

Vivian Tan (2013), Chinese schools offer primary education for urban refugees, UNHCR.

Kitty McKinsey (2017), Shanghai: Expo 2010 visitors peek into lives of refugees around the world, UNHCR.

Jessica Myers (2017), "China once welcomed refugees, but its policies now make Trump look lenient", Los Angles Times.

Preethi Amaresh (2017), "Terrorism and ethnicity crisis in China's Xinjiang Province", Chennai Centre for China Studies.

"North Korean defectors tend to be jobless, lag behind" (2015), Asia News.

Austin Ramzey (2015), "China and India are sitting out the refugee crisis", New York Times.

Anders Corr (2016), "Exclusive: Asian diplomat on Chinese role in Myanmar's Rohingya tragedy", *Forbes*.

Yimou Lee (2017), China draws three-stage path for Myanmar, Bangladesh to resolve Rohingya crisis, Reuters.

Bertil Lintner (2017), "A Chinese war in Myanmar", Asia Times.

Brent Crane (2015), "Kachin and China's troubled border", The Diplomat.

Jonathan Lesh (2017), "To Be a Global Leader, China Needs a New Refugee Policy", The Diplomat.

China to deploy drones in Xinjiang to prevent infiltration (2017), Economic Times.

Cunningham, Christopher P (2012), "Counter Terrorism in Xinjiang: The ETIM, China and Uyghurs", International Journal on world peace, JSTOR.

Martina, Michael "China's Xi says Xinjiang is front line on terrorism, hails police", *Reuters*, 29 April 2014.

"Xinjiang police fight the flow of guns, drugs and terrorist media from across border" (2017), Global Times.

" Who are the Uyghurs and why do they scare China"? (2016), Global Risk Insights.

Trinkle, Kate (2016), "China's New Silk Road and Its Impact on Xinjiang", *The Diplomat*.

Zhou, Zunyou (2016), "China's Comprehensive Counter-Terrorism Law", *The Diplomat*.

Monika, Chansoria (2017), "Anti-terror drive' is China's ruse to target Uyghurs", *Sunday Guardian Live*.

"China to deploy drones, wire fencing along Xinjiang border to prevent infiltration" (2017), Press Trust of India.

Blanchard, Ben (2017), "China's Xi calls for greater counter-terrorism cooperation with Turkey", Reuters.

Luqui, Rose and Yang, Fan (2017) "Anti-Muslim sentiment is on the rise in China", The Washington Post.

Tae-jun Kang (2020), "China Tightens Grips on North Korean Defectors", The Diplomat.

FP Editors (2019), "For Uighur Muslims in China, Life Keeps Getting Harder", Foreign Policy.

"Chinese hackers who pursued Uighurs also targeted Tibetans, researchers says" (2019), Japan Times.

Areeb Ullah (2019), **"Uighur refugees face deportation to China from Turkey", Middle East Eye.**

Scilla Alecci (2019), "How China Targets Uighurs 'One by One' for Using a Mobile App", International Consortium of Investigative Journalists.

Brian Hioe (2018), "Uighur refugees on the rise internationally", New bloom mag.

Omer Kanat (2018), "Uighur refugees deserve freedom", Bangkok Post.

"Chinese Uighurs in Saudi face impossible choice" (2020), Bangkok Post.

"Don't back Uighur abuse" (2019), Bangkok Post.

Molly Quell (2020), "Bulgaria Blocked From Deporting Uighur Muslims to China", Courthouse news

"China's police state goes global, leaving refugees in fear" (2019), New Strait Times.

"China took their parents: the Uighur refugee children of Turkey" (2019), New Strait Times.

Gill Bonnett (2020), "Uighur refugee who fled China left jobless while awaiting NZ residence", RNZ.

Colin P. Clarke and Paul Rexton Kan (2017), "Uighur Foreign Fighters:: An Under examined Jihadist Challenge", JSTOR

Stefanie Kam (2015), "Counter Terrorist Trends and Analyses, Vol. 7, No. 1", International Centre for Political Violence and Terrorism Research.

Anthony H. Cordesman (2017), "Global Trends in Terrorism", Center for Strategic and International Studies (CSIS).

Tong Zhao (2020), "Social Cohesion and Islamic Radicalization: Implications from the Uighur Insurgency", University of South Florida Board of Trustees.

Su Hao'En (2012), "Counter Terrorist Trends and Analyses, Vol. 4, No. 1", East Asia Country Assessment: China.

Ziad Haider (2005), "Sino-Pakistan Relations and Xinjiang's Uighurs: Politics, Trade, and Islam along the Karakoram Highway", University of California Press.

Rollie Lal, "Central Asia and Its Asian Neighbors", Security and Commerce at the Crossroads, RAND Corporation.

Justin M. Jacobs, "The birth pangs of Chinese affirmative action", Xinjiang and the Modern Chinese State, University of Washington Press.

Gideon Elazar (2017), "Moving Westward:: The Chinese Rebuilding of Syria", Begin-Sadat Center for Strategic Studies.

Dru C. Gladney, "Islam in China: Accommodation or Separation?", Religion in China, Major Concepts and Minority Positions, Austrian Academy of Sciences Press.

Wang Peng Xin and Sherali Yadgarov (2011), "Central and East Asia Country Assessments", International Centre for Political Violence and Terrorism Research.

Nodirbek Soliev (2017), "Uyghur militancy in and beyond Southeast Asia: An Assessment", International Centre for Political Violence and Terrorism Research.

Laura Steckman (2015), "Myanmar at the Crossroads: The Shadow of Jihadist Extremism", International Centre for Political Violence and Terrorism Research.

Kevin Sheives (2006), "China Turns West: Beijing's Contemporary Strategy Towards Central Asia", Pacific Affairs, University of British Columbia.

Malika Tukmadiyeva (2013),"Xinjiang in China's Foreign Policy toward Central Asia", Partnership for Peace Consortium of Defense Academies and Security Studies Institutes.

Rouben Azizian (2006), "Countering Islamic Radicalism in Central Asia", Partnership for Peace Consortium of Defense Academies and Security Studies Institutes.

Anthony H. Cordesman, Arleigh A. Burke and Max Molot (2019), China and Central Asia, Center for Strategic and International Studies (CSIS).

Nicolas Becquelin (2000), "Xinjiang in the Nineties", The China Journal

Angela Stanzel (2018), "Fear and loathing on the New Silk Road:: Chinese security in Afghanistan and beyond", European Council on Foreign Relations.

Paul Stronski and Richard Sokolsky (2020), "Multipolarity in Practice", Carnegie Endowment for International Peace.

"Chinas terrorism threat and response in 2016"(2017), Australian Strategic Policy Institute.

Chien-peng Chung (2004), "The Shanghai Co-operation Organization: China's Changing Influence in Central Asia", Cambridge University Press.

Andrew Mumford (2018), "Theory-Testing Uyghur Terrorism in China", Terrorism Research Initiative.

Justin M. Jacobs, "Imperial Repertoires in Republican Xinjiang", University of Washington Press.

Michael L. Zukosky (2012), "Quality, Development Discourse, and Minority Subjectivity in Contemporary Xinjiang", Modern China

James Millward (2004), "Violent Separatism in Xinjiang", East-West Center

Press Coverage of the Refugee and Migrant Crisis in the EU: A Content Analysis of Five European Countries, UNHCR.

Marianna Fotaki (2019), "A Crisis of Humanitarianism: Refugees at the Gates of Europe", International journal of health policy and management.

Is this humanitarian migration crisis different? (2015), OECD.

Lilie Chouliaraki (2015), "Rethinking humanity and responsibility in the refugee 'crisis': A visual typology of news media", London School of Economics and Political Science.

"Tackling the global refugee crisis" (2016), Amnesty International.

Alex Joffe and Asaf Romirowsky (2018), "Reframing the Middle Eastern and Palestinian Refugee Crises", Begin-Sadat Center for Strategic Studies.

Lester A. Zeager (2014), "Reconsidering the Prisoner's Dilemma Strategic Interaction in Refugee Negotiations", Georgetown University Press

Greg Philo, Emma Briant and Pauline Donald, "A Brief History of Contemporary Migration and Asylum",Bad News for Refugees, Pluto Press.

Gunther Beyer (1981), "The Political Refugee: 35 Years Later", The International Migration Review, Sage Publications, Inc.

Drew Thompson and Carla Freeman (2009), "China's Refugee Policies and Historic Treatment of Refugees", US-Korea Institute at SAIS.

Jeremy Hein (1993), "Refugees, Immigrants, and the State", JSTOR

Xavier Devictor and Quy-Toan Do (2017), "How Many Years Have Refugees Been in Exile?", Population Council, JSTOR

Aristide R. Zolberg, Astri Suhrke and Sergio Aguayo, "International Factors in the Formation of Refugee Movements", The International Migration Review, Sage Publications, Inc.

Oriana Skylar Mastro (2017), "China's Evolving North Korea Strategy", US Institute of Peace.

Rosemarie Rogers, "The Future of Refugee Flows and Policies", The International Migration Review, Sage Publications, Inc.

Refugee Law and Policy: China, The library of Congress.

Jane Golley, Linda Jaivin, Paul J. Farrelly and Sharon Strange, "The power of giving: China deepens involvement in refugee affairs", ANU Press.

Alison Brown, Peter Mackie, Kate Dickenson and Tegegne Gebre-Egziabher (2018), Urban refugee economies, International Institute for Environment and Development

Lili Song (2018), "China and the International Refugee Protection Regime: Past, Present, and Potentials", Oxford academic.

Jasmine Lam (2013), "China's Refugee Policy in Comparison", E-international relations.

Merriden Varrall (2017), "How China views the plight of refugees", Lowy Institute.

Jessica Meyers (2017), "China once welcomed refugees, but its policies now make Trump look lenient", Los Angeles Times.

Dong-ho Han (2011), "The Clash between Interest and Responsibility: China's Policy toward North Korean Escapees", The Korean Journal of Defense Analysis.

Song Lili, The Power of Giving: China Deepens Involvement in Refugee Affairs, The China Story.

Melvyn C. Goldstein and Cynthia M. Beall (1991), "China's Birth Control Policy in the Tibet Autonomous Region: Myths and Realities", University of California Press, JSTOR

UNHCR seeks cooperation with China within Belt and Road framework: UN official (2019), China daily

Francis Eve (2018), "The US withdrawal from the UNHRC is perfect for Xi Jinping and China", The Guardian.

Sanjana Ravi (2020), "Amid Coronavirus Spread, Host Countries Ignore Refugee Health at Their Own Peril", Foreign Policy.

More than 100 Chinese asylum seekers last year applied to NZ - UNHCR report, RNZ.

Richard Skretteberg (2018), "Ten things you should know about refugees from North Korea", Norwegian Refugee Council.

Shi Jiangtao (2017), "China willing to open its pockets, but not borders, to Middle East refugees", South China Morning Post.

Jonathan Lesh (2017), "To Be a Global Leader, China Needs a New Refugee Policy", The Diplomat.

Reuters Staff (2017), "China says it will make efforts on Syria reconstruction", Reuters.

Tom O'Connor (2017), "China Will Not Accept Syrian Refugees Because It Wants Them to Return Home", Newsweek

Refugees and internally displaced persons, Central Intelligence Agency.

Efforts to Tackle Global Displacement Crisis 'Fragmented', Refugee Agency Chief Tells Security Council, Saying They Address Mere Symptoms, Not Root Causes (2019), United Nations.

Fleeing Home: Refugees and Human Trafficking (2019), Council on foreign relations.

Michael R. Pompeo, Secretary of State, Russian Federation's and China's Veto of UNSCR 2449 Aid to Syrian Refugees, U.S department of State.

Sarah Jackson-Han (2009), "Kokang Fighters Flee to China", Radio Free Asia

C. S. Kuppuswamy (2015), "MYANMAR: The War with the Kokangs", South Asia Analysis

Luisetta Mudie (2015), "Kokang Army Recruiting Chinese Nationals as Mercenaries in Yunnan: Sources", Radio Free Asia.

"Thousands flee clashes between army and rebels in Myanmar" (2015), BBC news

"No relaxation of citizenship law for Kokang: minister" (2016), The Myanmar Times

Shi Jiangtao (2017), "Why China is willing to open its pockets, but not its borders, to Middle Eastern refugees", South China Morning Post

Giorgio Cafiero (2020), "China plays the long game on Syria", Middle East Institute

John. J Catherine (2018), "China completes $2 million program for Syrian refugees in Kurdistan", Kurdistan 24

China's Position on Syria Issue, Embassy of People's Republic of China in the Republic of Botswana.

Wang Jin (2017), "Why Do Chinese Reject Middle Eastern Refugees?", The Diplomat

John Calabrese (2019), "China and Syria: In War and Reconstruction", Middle East Institute

Isaac Kfir (2020), "China vies for role in reconstructing Syria", Asia and the Pacific Policy Society

K Yhome (2019), "Understanding China's response to ethnic conflicts in Myanmar", Observer Research Foundation

James Pomfret (2017), "Relief camp in China swells as thousands flee conflict in Myanmar", Reuters

"Syrian refugees profoundly hit by COVID-19 economic downturn" (2020), UNHCR

"Impact of COVID-19 on Syrian refugees and host communities in Jordan and Lebanon" (2020), International Labor Organization

"The Middle-Way Policy", Central Tibetan Administration

Mary Hui (2020), "China's election to the UN Human Rights Council revealed its shaky global status", Quartz Edvard Hambro (1957), "Chinese Refugees in Hong Kong", Clark Atlanta University

Michael Ramsden (2014), "Refugees in Hong Kong: Developing the legal framework for socio-economic rights protection.

Gordon Mathews (2018), "Asylum Seekers as Symbols of Hong Kong's Non-Chineseness", China Perspectives

Alexander Betts, Gil Loescher and James Milner, 2nd Edition, "UNHCR: The Politics and Practice of Refugee Protection, Global Institutions

Edited by Elena Fiddian-Qasmiyeh, Gil Loescher, Katy Long, and Nando Sigona, The Oxford Handbook of Refugees and Forced Migration Studies

Edited by Anna Triandafyllidou, "Routledge Handbook of Immigration and Refugee Studies", Routledge International Handbooks

Edited by Alexander Betts and Gil Loescher, "Refugees in International Relations", Oxford

Collection of International Instruments and Legal Texts Concerning Refugees and others of Concern to UNHCR (2007), UNHCR

Words for Index

A

Africa, 15-16, 24, 43, 74, 93-94

Al Qaeda, 58, 65

Amnesty International, 17, 63, 95, 110

Arakan, 84-85

asylum, 16, 20-21, 24-26, 32-33, 36, 51-52, 67, 90-91, 93-96, 101, 110, 112, 114

Atharvaveda, 42

Aung San Suu Kyi, 79-80, 85

B

Bandung, 42

Bangladesh, 84-86, 106

Beijing, 21, 24, 61-62, 66, 78, 87, 102, 109

below the poverty line, 39

Belt and Road Initiative (BRI), 24

British, 67, 70-71, 78, 84, 90, 95, 109

Buddhism, 42, 44-45

Burma, 11, 70-72, 75, 84-86

C

Central Asia, 57, 59-62, 66, 108-109

China, 1, 5, 7, 9-12, 15, 18-22, 24-27, 30-33, 36-39, 42-48, 50-54, 56-67, 70-75, 78-81, 86-87, 90-91, 93-96, 98-114

Cold War, 9, 50, 52

Confucianism, 103-104

Confucius, 103

COVID-19, 7, 17, 39, 99-100, 113

Cultural Revolution, 20, 53, 57

D

Dalai Lama, 15, 42-44, 46-47

Deng Xiaoping, 21, 42, 57, 100

Displacement, 14, 16, 20, 24, 26, 112

Dungan Revolt, 56

E

Emigration, 30, 36, 52

Europe, 9, 16, 24, 36, 38, 57, 59, 67, 110

Extremism, 61, 63, 109

G

Geneva, 31, 37, 46-47, 103

Genocide, 12, 67, 84

Global conflict, 47

Global security, 15

Globalization, 9, 22

Golden Crescent, 59

Great Leap forward, 20, 57

H

Han Chinese, 43, 56, 63, 65

Hong Kong, 5, 9-11, 20, 30-32, 39, 47, 89-96, 100, 102, 114

Human Rights, 11-12, 14, 43, 46-47, 51-53, 64, 67, 70-71, 74, 85-87, 94-96, 103, 105, 114

I

Immigration, 43, 52, 80, 85, 91, 93, 101, 103, 114

imperialism, 43

India, 7, 9, 15, 42-44, 46, 56, 70, 84-85, 99, 106-107

Indochina, 10, 30

Intergovernmental organizations, 14

International Committee of the Red Cross, 11, 38

International Court of Justice (ICJ), 25

International law, 22, 26, 47-48, 51, 84, 98

International organizations, 11, 14, 17, 87

International treaties, 14

J

Japan, 20, 32, 91, 103, 107

Jawaharlal Nehru, 7, 10, 43

jihadists, 57, 61-62

K

Kachin, 5, 11, 69-75, 79-81, 105-106

Khunjerab, 58-59

Kokang, 5, 10, 77-81, 105, 112-113

Korean peninsula, 50, 54

L

liberalization, 63, 71

M

Mao Zedong, 20, 42, 98

Middle East, 36-37, 39, 57, 74, 107, 112-113

migration, 9, 30-32, 43, 56, 73, 90-91, 110-111, 114

military, 20, 42, 47, 60, 70-71, 85, 98, 101

Mount Kailash, 42

Myanmar, 9-11, 16, 21, 70-75, 78-81, 84-87, 102, 105-106, 109, 113

N

Nation-states, 14, 56, 101

Nepal, 10, 43

North Korea, 5, 10, 49-54, 111-112

O

Olympics, 54

Open door policy, 21

P

Palestine, 15-16
Pyongyang, 53-54

Q

Qing dynasty, 42, 56, 90

R

racism, 93-94
Rakhine, 84-87
Rangoon, 70
Refugee Convention, 24-26, 51-52, 73, 75, 81, 90, 92, 101
refugee status determinations, 12, 22
resettlement, 14, 27, 30-33, 36, 45, 53, 87, 91, 102
Rigveda, 42
Rohingya, 5, 16, 26, 83-87, 102-103, 106

S

Separatism, 57-59, 61, 110
Shan State, 74, 78-79
Shanghai Cooperation Organization, 12, 61
Sinification, 45
South Korea, 51-54
South-East Asia, 30
South East Asia, 30, 94
Soviet union, 15, 52, 63, 100
Suez Canal, 38

Switzerland, 47-48
Syria, 5, 10, 16, 21, 35-39, 65-66, 108, 112-113

T

Taiwan, 9, 20, 58, 94, 100
Terrorist, 12, 38, 58-59, 61, 64, 106, 108
Tibet, 5, 10, 41-48, 58, 111
Turkey, 16, 38, 66-67, 107-108

U

UNHCR, 5, 7, 12, 14, 18, 20-27, 31-32, 36, 39, 52-53, 73, 75, 79, 81, 85-86, 91-94, 102-103, 105, 110, 112-114
United Nations, 7, 12, 14-15, 21, 84, 112
United Nations Relief and Works Agency (UNRWA), 15
UNSC, 12, 20, 38, 70-71, 102
Uyghurs, 38-39, 43, 47, 56-67, 106-107

V

Vietnam, 26, 30-32, 91, 102

W

War, 9, 14-16, 20, 32, 36, 38-39, 50-52, 56-57, 71, 84-85, 90-91, 99-101, 106, 113
World Bank, 38
World Food Program, 12, 38
World Health Organization, 12, 38

World War II, 14, 32, 84

X

Xi Jinping, 21, 37, 45, 65, 98, 101, 112

Xinjiang, 5, 10, 12, 39, 45, 47, 55-68, 106-110

Y

Yunnan, 31, 70-75, 78-81, 105, 113

Z

Zhou Enlai, 42